WISE UP AND BE
THE SOLUTION

WISE UP AND BE THE SOLUTION

How to Create a Culture of Learning at Home and Make Your Child a Success in School

James L. Casale, PhD

Skyhorse Publishing

Visit our website at www.skyhorsepublishing.com.

10 9 8 7 6 5 4 3 2 1

Library of Congress Cataloging-in-Publication Data is available on file.

Cover photo credit: Thinkstock

Print ISBN: 978-1-63450-408-9
Ebook ISBN: 978-1-63450-880-3

Printed in the United States of America

"You know more than you think you do."
—Benjamin Spock

CONTENTS

Any success I have enjoyed on this planet, I owe to my parents, Frank and Carmel Casale. They are the inspiration for this book. Their love, loyalty, devotion, selflessness, and faith guided me in my desire to never disappoint them.

To my children James and Karen, who have become exceptional parents.

To all the parents who toil daily to provide a loving and learning environment for their children.

ACKNOWLEDGMENTS

I thank my wife, Janet, for her love and her support of this project. Her understanding of the peculiarities of the struggling writer, a novice one at that, helped propel me to the finish line.

My editor, Donna Carbone, was invaluable to this exercise, not merely for her editing expertise, but for the insights she provided on a topic that is dear to her heart. Her own experiences as a parent, writer, and keen observer of schools and schooling added immeasurably to the clarity of all the concepts presented in my book.

Soon after I arrived in Naples, Florida, in 1969, I met the best mentor any teacher could hope for, Mary Cunningham. Not only was she a gifted teacher of elementary and middle school students, she inspired her colleagues with a dedication to learn more, take risks, and always try to be better tomorrow than they were today. She was the consummate reflective teacher, who co-taught with me and inspired me to be a lifelong learner and a lifelong student.

In 2013, I celebrated fifty years in my beloved profession. It would require another book to acknowledge the many students and parents who have rewarded me with their insights, loyalty, and support. They have provided learning opportunities that could never be acquired in a college classroom.

I am indebted to my colleagues—the teachers and administrators too numerous to mention—who have dedicated their art to helping children succeed. They are integral to every chapter in this book.

Second only to inspiring students to learn more and do more was the privilege of hiring teachers who have gone on to excel at their craft and provide their students, parents, school, and community with our nation's most valuable resource—highly effective teaching.

I will be forever grateful to the staff at Purchase Elementary School and the staff at Preston Elementary School for their loyalty, support, and uncanny ability to make me look good as their school principal.

PART 1: TAKING AN ACTIVE ROLE

"It is a greater work to educate a child . . . than to rule a state."

—William Ellery Channing

"It's not about you"[1] is the first line of the first chapter of one of the most popular books of the twenty-first century—Rick Warren's *The Purpose Driven Life*. Throughout my time as a school principal, I have never forgotten it. The book encourages readers to live a life that serves others.

The decision to become a parent carries with it a responsibility and requires a devotion and commitment like no other. Who else could be charged with the unrelenting task of loving, nurturing, protecting, and teaching another human being from birth to adulthood and doing it unselfishly? Certainly not presidents or generals or clergy or scientists; not writers or poets—no one but you, the parent, can preside over the life you created.

No one is more important or influential to your child than you are, and no task is more important than the one you have chosen. Why should or would anyone care more about your child than you do? Your child is your legacy and the future of our world. Parents are the first mediators of the culture of a growing child.

"A child is a person who is going to carry on what you have started. He will assume control of your cities, states, and nations. He is going to move in and take over your churches, schools, corporations. . . . The fate of humanity is in his hands."

—Abraham Lincoln

There is little need for me to repeat here what researchers have been consistently saying for many decades: parents are the most important influence on their child's emotional, psychological, physical, and academic growth. They are their children's first and foremost teachers.

As a principal, I learned that children's success in school was closely correlated to the nature of their lives outside of its walls. Considering that students spend most of their time outside the classroom, it becomes obvious that their growth and development hinge primarily on the learning environment—I prefer *learning culture*—that parents establish in their homes.

Even back in 1966, the *Coleman Report* concluded that the best predictor of a child's performance in school is the quality of the family from which he or she comes. A child's achievement is *not* based on the money and resources families possess. It's about the determination parents possess to establish their own learning environment.

Not long ago, an NBA player changed his name to The Answer. He wasn't. He did not inspire. He did not lead. He was about showmanship and bravado and talked a "good game," but he did not back up his words with actions.

When it comes to your child's education, the most powerful and influential names on that team are Mom and Dad. They are the coaches, and home is the training facility.

THE TEACHING PROFESSION AND PARENTS

> "If a doctor, lawyer, or dentist had forty people in his office at one time, all of whom had different needs, and some of whom did not want to be there and were causing trouble, and the doctor, lawyer, or dentist, without assistance, had to treat them all with professional excellence for nine months, then he might have some conception of the classroom teacher's job."
>
> —Donald D. Quinn

Highly effective teachers are worth their weight in diamonds because that's what they are. They sparkle, dazzle, and amaze us with their artistry. They are beautiful to behold. I have been an educator for fifty years. I have taught at every level of public education, from elementary grades to graduate school. I have also been an administrator at the elementary, middle school, and district levels. My teaching and leadership roles have led me to positions in four states. I have learned firsthand that there are not enough highly effective teachers or principals to go around. The shortage of highly effective teachers and administrators is well known and is the root cause of school reform and parent dissatisfaction.

Parents are not expected to be professional teachers, nor do they need to be. This book will *not* direct you to design elaborate learning activities or to teach reading, math, or science. This book is *not* about homeschooling, although it will enhance the efforts of parents who have taken on that responsibility. Establishing a learning culture in your home and being a positive force in your child's education does *not* require any special skills.

This book will steer parents toward developing a positive attitude, becoming committed to their responsibility, gaining some basic knowledge, and being proactive. As I like to say:

Knowledge is power and influence; becoming proactive increases both.

A useful analogy on gaining knowledge and being proactive can be found when dealing with health issues. While you are not expected to become as knowledgeable as a doctor, you are expected to learn as much as you can about maintaining your own health and improving the quality of your life. This knowledge will also assist you in asking the right questions and making better decisions when faced with a medical problem.

This same idea applies to educating your child. Do not, under any circumstances, rely solely on teachers, principals, or other school personnel for information. Develop your own knowledge base about educational matters. You will be better informed and more confident in the decisions you make for your child.

None of this negates your efforts to work cooperatively and collaboratively with teachers and staff. Visit your child's school at the beginning of each academic year and meet the teachers who will be guiding your child's education. Make it clear that you are open to suggestions and advice. Establish and maintain regular and positive contact with the teacher, and consider the teacher an important factor in your efforts to create an optimal learning environment at home. A caring, interested, and knowledgeable parent can become the teacher's best assistant. Teachers and parents have a mutual interest in student success and should become allies, not adversaries.

WHAT SHOULD PARENTS KNOW AND BE ABLE TO DO?

First, let's dispel the myth of perfection. There are no perfect teachers and no perfect parents. Raising children can be rewarding, fun, fulfilling, satisfying, and uplifting. It can also be tedious, time-consuming, bumpy, nerve-racking, downright scary, painful, and pockmarked with failures and setbacks. If you are a parent, I'm not telling you anything you don't already know.

Have you ever met a parent who did not want his or her child to succeed in school and life? Of course not! Since knowledge is power—and results in influence—parents need to acquire accurate information about what constitutes a learning culture at home and devise a plan to make it a reality.

FUELING YOUR EFFORTS

In his wildly successful book, *The 7 Habits of Highly Effective People*, Stephen Covey listed the habit of being proactive as the first and most important element of success.[2] I will take the liberty of amending Dr. Covey's words for this book by adding, "Become knowledgeable and then become proactive."

If you are not at least minimally knowledgeable about how kids learn before you begin, you will appear ignorant or, worse, stupid. Of course, along the way, while you are charting your course and carrying out your plans, your kids will, at one time or another, think that—"*Duh!*"—you are all of the above and more. Don't give them any ammunition.

Throughout this book, I will encourage you to remain attentive, confident, civil, and proactive. Accomplishing your goals requires an attitude adjustment. Study after study concludes that attitudes about learning—both your attitude and your child's attitude—profoundly affect success. Adopt a mindset based on the following points, and hold on to it like a life raft.

- Learning is important.
- Education is important.

- School is important.
- Experiences outside of school are important.
- Reading is essential.
- Always striving to do your best is critical.

These beliefs provide the fuel for your efforts. They're your mantra.

One of our first lessons as parents, one that we learn very quickly, is that we cannot make children do anything they don't want to do. Aside from torture, coercion, bribes, canceling cable and all electronics, or making your child listen to Yanni, your chances of forcing your child to read a book are slim to none. You can, however, provide the setting wherein your child may want to read something.

I vividly remember an episode at my dinner table when I thought I could force my nine-year-old son to eat his peas. "You're not leaving this table until you eat those peas," I threatened. We sat for a long time. So did the peas. It seemed like an eternity passed. My son never uttered a word, never talked back. He did make faces and expressions that were easily interpreted as, *Yeah, right!* or, *You can't make me eat those stinking, smelly green pebbles*. He was right. He didn't eat them. Life goes on, but not without some compromise.

I changed *my* attitude. Hey, *I* don't even like peas. In fact, I don't remember ever eating peas unless they were encased in my father's incomparable tomato sauce, while mingling with garlic, onions, and elbow macaroni. In my house, this dish was known as pasta pezzelle. Now my son likes pasta pezzelle. He eats peas.

SET THE TABLE OR BE THE GARDENER

No, you can't force your child to eat peas or read books, but you can set the table. Provide an environment for learning in your home, and good things will happen. Your child will eventually come to the table—in this case, the learning table.

The learning table is a house filled with good books, regular routines, family discussions, quiet places, and parents who model their expectations. It's a house that limits use of TV, computer time—unless it's educational—video games, and cell phones. It's a house characterized by selflessness, love, patience, humor, civility, perseverance, hard work, and kindness.

A gardener does not make plants grow. A gardener prepares the soil with the best organic materials, provides water and sunlight, and hopes for the best crop. Consider yourself a gardener, and create a learning garden with superior ingredients. This book will inspire you and provide the tools and fertile soil you need for your learning garden.[3]

OUR FAILING SCHOOLS

> "Schools don't belong to the employees; they belong to the parents and taxpayers."
>
> —James L. Casale

A significant amount of research reveals that our public schools, generally speaking, are inferior. The year 2013 marked the thirtieth anniversary of the landmark report *A Nation at Risk,* released in 1983 by the National Commission on Excellence in Education. The report declared that the "educational foundations of our society are presently being eroded by a rising tide of mediocrity that threatens our very future as a nation and a people."[4]

Where are we today? A recent report in *Education Week* reveals stagnant reading and math scores. The report also includes the results of a Gallup poll indicating that confidence in the public schools has declined from 39 percent in 1983 to 29 percent in 2012.

There are not enough highly effective teachers, and leaders are in short supply. The talent pool is shallow and always has been. Teachers' unions are obstacles to reform. While they have served their membership admirably by raising salaries and fighting for better working conditions, they continue to resist change, cling to the status quo and defend lifetime jobs known as tenure. Some union representatives in Florida claim that child poverty, underfunded schools, inadequate pay, over-regulation and misguided accountability are the real culprits responsible for harming public education. They make a good point about inadequate pay, but those who chose our profession know that when they sign up. And it supports the reasons for why we don't attract the best and the brightest. Also, with few exceptions, poor teachers make the same money as the best teachers. This is not a system that will ever attract the best and the brightest. School budgets have always been heavily skewed toward salaries, but more money has never been the answer except for politicians who are trying to get elected. Additionally, state legislators are uninformed, unreliable, and usually make political decisions based on special interests.

The reform movement has been and is inspired by parents—parents who are fed up and dissatisfied with a system that has failed their children. They have changed the dynamic. The result of this disappointment has been a proliferation of charter schools, voucher programs, homeschooling, and virtual schooling.

We are currently reading more and more about governors and state legislators who are reform-minded, and who have significantly expanded charter schools and voucher programs in their states. These forward-thinking politicians recognize the effect that inferior public schools have on children, parents, society, and real estate. With each succeeding school year, there are more parent requests for charter schools and vouchers to attend private schools. There is no magic in these options other than they provide hope for beleaguered parents.

Arthur Levine is a former president of Columbia University Teachers College. In an article he wrote for the *Wall Street Journal,* "The Suburban Education Gap," he asserts that even suburban school districts are losing ground and merely settling in on a "path of global mediocrity." He emphasizes, "This isn't a game for amateurs. Parents need to use every resource at their disposal—demanding changes in schools and in district offices; using existing tools such as 'parent trigger' laws and charter schools, organizing their communities . . . and telling politicians and office holders that their votes will go to candidates who support improvement."[5]

Joel Klein, the former chancellor of the New York City Public Schools, posits views that are also contrary to union positions and our teacher training colleges. In his recent book, *Lessons of Hope: How to Fix Our Schools,* Klein reveals that economically challenged parents deserve options for their children, smaller schools are better than large schools, the self-esteem movement does not provide the tools and knowledge kids need, teacher preparation programs are weak, and teachers unions are obstructionists to progress.

Klein's views are not a surprise because they are not new. My five decades in public education are a testament to the solid truths espoused by Klein. His criticisms have always been part of the education landscape. Highly effective teaching is not the norm and never will be. Improving the quality of teaching on a grand scale is a losing proposition, because as Klein reminds us, teacher's colleges resist change and their standards are low.

But let's not get into a blame game before we—the parents—examine what we are doing. Many schools and their teachers try hard to do the best they can for your child. Are you doing the best you can for your child? Parents—even the so-called educated ones—are capable of being lazy, apathetic, and ignorant or, heaven forbid, all three. Imagine the progress in education and a child's school and life success if parents embraced their role as their child's first teacher and role model.

This book is designed to challenge, provoke, and inspire parents to become more knowledgeable, committed, and active in establishing a learning culture in their homes. Parents are *not* required to have any special skills or specific training. The requirements that will lead to success are motivation, a positive attitude, a mission statement that briefly describes the goals for your family that emphasize self-restraint, compassion, kindness, sharing, respect and responsibility. Couple these with acquiring accurate information about schools and a plan of action. Now we have "Lessons in Hope."

> "A teacher affects eternity; no one can tell where his influence stops."
>
> —Henry Adams

My apologies, Mr. Adams, but may I offer the following amendment? A *parent* affects eternity; no one can tell where her or his influence stops.

CHAPTER 1: ATTITUDE

"'Tis education forms the mind: just as the twig is bent, the tree's inclined."

—Alexander Pope

My father wore my brother's high school ring because he wanted people to think he had graduated from high school. My mother, who was forced to leave school at the age of sixteen to become a seamstress, was not as self-conscious about her lack of formal education. She did, however, share his attitude about school and schooling. The "motivational" speech they most often drummed into my siblings and me went something like this:

"Getting an education is important. School is important. You go to school even if you don't feel like it. You will take school seriously and do well. You are going to college."

Those words ended my dream of becoming a Good Humor man or the next Mickey Mantle. My brother, two sisters, and I knew that my parents were not just speaking to hear themselves talk. They were issuing a mandate.

Mom and Dad had high expectations for their children. They both worked full time, which prevented them from attending school conferences or open houses. I never asked my parents to help me with my homework, and they never offered. They trusted me to complete my assignments as my teachers instructed. Although they did not actively participate at school or help with homework, they were never ambivalent about the importance of achieving a formal education. They taught responsibility and hard work by example. We learned well; we did not want to ever disappoint them.

THE FIRST STEP

Developing a strong, positive attitude about the importance and value of education is your first step in creating a learning laboratory in your home. My friend Danny reminded me that *attitude* is a gift you give to yourself. It coalesces with your belief system and underpins what you are trying to accomplish. Not only does attitude need to be infused into your plan of action, it is the foundation of your plan of action.

Your positive attitude about the value of education and the behavior you model will influence the perceptions acquired by your child. This is fundamental to the lifelong learning trip expected from your child.

Our failures as parents can often be traced to our own shortcomings: apathy, carelessness, selfishness, laziness, and, worst of all, ignorance. Your decision to become a parent carries with it a faith and a trust that you *will* do the right thing. Your children didn't choose you; you chose them.

HOPES AND DREAMS

From one of the great American musicals, *Carousel*, the song "Soliloquy" reveals the hopes and dreams of a prospective dad. The lyrics, by Oscar Hammerstein, include these words:

But he'll have more common sense
Than his pudding-headed father ever had
I'll teach him to wrestle and dive through a wave
When we go in the morning for our swim
His mother can teach him
The way to behave
But she won't make a sissy out o' him . . . .

I don't give a damn what he does
As long as he does what he likes!
He can sit on his tail
Or work on a rail
With a hammer, hammering spikes!
He can ferry a boat on a river
Or peddle a pack on his back
Or work up and down
The streets of a town
With a whip and a horse and a hack[1]

What are your hopes and dreams for your child? Think about them, sort them out, and write them down. They will become the framework for your belief system, your written pledge or mission statement, and, lastly, your plan of action. They will provide you with a clearer and more manageable direction.

This basic foundation becomes the formula for your commitment to love, nurture, teach, and protect your child. It has to be as solid as the Matterhorn.

WHAT DO I WANT FOR MY CHILD?

How many times have you heard, "I want my child to be a doctor"? This is often followed by, in no particular order, teacher, lawyer, carpenter, scientist, entrepreneur, plumber, president, athlete, actor, journalist, engineer, architect, or comedian. Then there is this statement, made by parents who imagine themselves to be less controlling: "I just want him to be happy doing what he loves." What if what he loves is something you hate?

> "I never wanted this for you, Michael. I wanted you to be Senator Corleone or President Corleone."
> —Marlon Brando as Vito Corleone, *The Godfather, Part One*

Do not waste your time and energy thinking about careers, occupations, wealth, or prestige. Even in the best of circumstances, you may have little control over the final decision your child makes about a career or a direction in life. Remember; set the table or be the gardener.

Expend your time and energy on your commitment and dedication to being the best parent you can be, while guiding your child along the path of lifelong learning. Wear a hard hat. You may need it.

The road ahead will be rife with uneven surfaces. Expect twists, turns, hairpin curves, hills, and valleys. Detours and barricades will block the way from time to time. Stay focused! Keep your eye on the endgame. Remain committed to raising your child in a culture of learning that supports her social, emotional, physical, and intellectual growth, and you, too, will arrive at your destination wiser for the journey.

Let's put thoughts of occupations and careers aside for the time being. Think back to the days immediately after your child was born. What were you thinking as you cuddled your infant in your arms and peered lovingly into his or her face?

Were you hoping she would become president, or did your thoughts center on whether she would become an honest, caring, responsible, and compassionate person? How about healthy, kind, and respectful? My guess is, you wished for all of these and more.

Most likely, the things you wished for your child were the things you hold most dear in your own life. Your personal beliefs will direct and guide you as you maneuver through the long stretches of your child's journey: infancy, toddlerhood, childhood, adolescence, and—gasp!—adulthood.

> "For the hand that rocks the cradle
> Is the hand that rules the world."
> —William Ross Wallace

CHAPTER 2: I PLEDGE ALLEGIANCE

"What greater or better gift can we offer the republic than to teach and instruct our youth?"

—Cicero

I pledge allegiance to the flag of the United States of America and to the republic for which it stands, one nation under God, indivisible, with liberty and justice for all.

How often have you recited the Pledge of Allegiance? The answer, most likely, would be too many times to estimate. How often have you stopped to consider what the words mean?

Medical doctors swear allegiance to the Hippocratic Oath when they become licensed. Boy Scouts hold up the three middle fingers of their right hand to take their oath. Witnesses in a court trial place their hand on a bible and swear to tell the truth, the whole truth, and nothing but the truth.

Pledges and oaths, slogans and mottos and mission statements are acknowledgments of loyalty, dedication, and purpose. They pervade every aspect of our society. Swearing-in ceremonies are conducted by our local, state, and national governments, our military, clubs and civic organizations and corporations. Corporate slogans that bombard your television screen are easily recognizable. Allstate Insurance reminds you ad nauseam that "you're in good hands."

Your school most likely has its own motto or slogan. Do you know what it is? Your school district and/or school have mission statements. Can you paraphrase them? Some examples are below.

School Slogans and Mottoes:
- A Family of Learners
- The Future Begins Here
- Knowledge Is Power
- Committed to Lifelong Learning

Military Slogans and Mottoes:
- Marines: *Semper Fidelis*—Always Faithful
- Army: An Army of One
- Coast Guard: *Semper Paratus*—Always Prepared

Corporate Slogans:
- Nike: JUST DO IT.
- Verizon: Can you hear me now?
- Toyota: Oh what a *feeling*!

School Mission Statements:
- Princeton Academy of the Sacred Heart (Princeton, New Jersey): "Our mission is to develop young men with creative and active minds, a sense of understanding and compassion for others, and the courage to act on their beliefs. We stress the total development of each child: spiritual, moral, intellectual, social, emotional, and physical."
- Community School (Roanoke, Virginia): "Community School recognizes that each child is an individual; that all children are creative; that all children need to succeed.

Therefore, Community School respects the individual needs of children; fosters a caring and creative environment; and emphasizes the social, emotional, physical, and intellectual development of each child."[1]

The commonalities are obvious. This is not quantum physics. You can easily create a mission statement for your home that specifies your hopes, dreams, expectations and beliefs. Think of your family as an organization whose total membership is confined to you, your spouse, and your children. Now, promote your purpose and beliefs.

Aspiring entrepreneurs often get advice: *Focus on your mission. Write a clear mission statement to help you stay on track.*

As parents, we can benefit from this kind of focus, too. We must accept the enormous challenge that is inherent in bringing children into the world. And we must take a personal oath that promises to love, teach, guide, nurture, and protect our precious offspring as best we can.

From infancy to adulthood, we hold on to our dreams and hopes that our children will be happy, healthy, successful, and fulfilled. And, as Winston Churchill said, "Never, never, never, never, give up."

I encourage parents to prepare a written statement that frames their hopes, dreams and expectations for their children. Whether you call it a pledge or mission statement, it need consist of only a few sentences that reveal your purpose for turning your home into a loving and caring learning environment.

Pride may be one of the seven deadly sins when taken to excess, but family pride can serve as a positive motivator for all family members. Pride is often promoted within companies, teams, schools, and the military—The Few, The Proud, The Marines. Pride can complement your efforts to achieve your family mission.

THE PLEDGE OR MISSION STATEMENT

The premise of this book is that parents are children's first and most important teacher. They wield enormous influence over whether or not their children will blossom, become self-sufficient and reach their potential.

Here are some simple steps to help you write your own pledge or mission statement:

1. Determine what is most important regarding your child's future and write it down.
2. Create a formal document. Frame it and hang it conspicuously in your home.
3. Discuss it with your family.
4. Understand that this document may change with time. Modify it if necessary.
5. Remain calm, committed, courageous and consistent.

If you falter, remember this quote from Oscar Wilde: "Experience is the name everyone gives to their mistakes."

A Sample Pledge

I pledge allegiance to parenthood and the responsibility and accountability that it requires. I promise to love, nurture, teach, and protect my child by being a caring parent and a role model. I will establish a culture of learning in my home that is characterized by love, kindness, respect, responsibility, and hard work.

Your pledge represents your belief system and drives your plan of action. The remaining chapters will offer basic knowledge and useful suggestions that will guide you through the formulation of a plan and assist you with solid decision making. The goal is to help your child succeed in life and school.

A Sample Mission Statement

Our mission as a family is to create a learning environment that is characterized by love, respect, kindness, and responsibility. Our home will be a safe, orderly, and supportive place that emphasizes the social, emotional, physical, and intellectual growth of each member.

Create a pledge or a mission statement. If you need help putting your beliefs into a prepared statement, search online or at the library. Speak with education professionals you know and respect. Keep it simple, clear, and brief.

"If your vision is for a year, plant wheat.
If your vision is for ten years, plant trees.
If your vision is for a lifetime, plant people."
—Chinese proverb

CHAPTER 3: SAFETY AND SECURITY

"The desire for safety stands against every great and noble enterprise."
—Tacitus

The alarm clock sounds. Another school day begins. The kids not only are awake and up, but are washed and dressed. They eat breakfast and then—yippee!—brush their teeth. Backpacks in hand, they are ready to roll. You walk them to the bus stop or drive them to school and wave good-bye. As they fade from your sight, you shout, "Have a great day!"

When you said, "Have a great day!"—what were you thinking about? Did any of the following thoughts enter your mind?

- I hope they learn something.
- I hope they stay out of trouble and eat their lunch.
- I hope they are not harmed in any way.

This book is about the environment you create at home, but you cannot always control what goes on outside of it. This chapter is a guide to doing your very best to make your child as safe and secure as possible.

WHICH OF THESE IS A PRIORITY?

Of course you hope they have a great day, a productive day, a day that includes learning and developing and maturing as they interact with their teachers and their peers and contend with their school's normal routines and demands. But the primary concern of every parent is the safety and security of his or her children. What parents expect, even if they don't consciously think about it, is that their children will enter a school environment that is caring, supportive, protective, and free from risks or threats.

As a teacher and a principal, I observed what I came to realize was a daily "routine" that many parents followed when they brought their child to school: they watched. Whether they walked their child to the school door or remained in the car, they watched their child until he or she was safely inside the building. While this behavior may be more common at the elementary level, it underscores a critical concern for all parents: personal safety. Parents need assurance themselves that their children arrive at school unharmed. Are you confident that the safety and security rules, regulations, and protocols set forth by your school and school district are comprehensive enough to ensure a safe, productive, and healthy learning environment for your child?

We are all aware of the harmful and sometimes violent incidents that take place around the country at every level of academic life, from elementary schools to college campuses. Although you recognize that accidents can and will happen in spite of the most thoughtful and comprehensive planning, your knowledge of and participation in school safety and security will be both useful and reassuring to you.

Even if you are confident that your school is a safe and secure place, familiarize yourself with school and district documents that outline safety and security information, volunteer for committees, chaperone at school events, observe, and ask questions.

Safety protocols range from the physical presence of police and security personnel, metal detectors, bag checks, and pat-downs to less stringent tactics, which may include locked entry doors, buzzer systems, and sign-in sheets. The school's location often dictates the safety protocols in place, but no school is immune from the potential for danger.

I became the principal of Purchase School in Harrison, New York, in 1984. The school was located at the intersection of two well-traveled roads and not in a residential area. Immediately after I was hired, staff members and parents informed me that our school was a hub for people seeking directions to surrounding towns and businesses. In the beginning of my tenure, I discovered quickly that our exterior doors were kept unlocked. It was not unusual for me or my staff to find strangers wandering the hallways, seeking directions to nearby locations. Thankfully, there were no incidents, but I was determined to shut down the "AAA expectations" my office staff was enduring and boost security at the same time. Subsequently, all exterior doors were locked at a designated time and a buzzer system was installed that alerted office personnel when someone requested entry.

The following safety and security measures, in no particular order, represent what many school districts across the country have implemented. While the list may not be totally comprehensive, I hope it will serve as a guide for parents and provoke thinking about the best ways to keep our children out of harm's way.

COMPONENTS OF A SAFE AND SECURE SCHOOL

If you are concerned about school safety and security—as you should be, given the current state of affairs—obtain a copy of the state level, district level and school level documents that outline safety and security measures and protocols.

Read the documents thoroughly and take notes if questions arise in your mind. Read for answers to the following questions:

- Who authored the document? Were the community's first responders—police, fire rescue and EMS—consulted and asked to contribute their ideas?
- Did the school district do their research to create plans that are comprehensive and current?
- Are there district level and school level safety and security committees that meet regularly to evaluate and modify the existing plans?
- Are all staff members, professional, non-professional and volunteers, trained to respond accordingly to situations that occur?

Schools around the country employ a variety of safety and security measures, often dependent on their neighborhoods. For example, inner-city schools may opt for on-campus security personnel, cameras, and metal detectors, while suburban and rural schools choose less stringent methods such as buzzer systems, sign-in logs and ID tags for all staff and visitors. However, violent and unpredictable incidents can happen in any location and are not confined to inner city schools or high-crime areas.

The terms *safety* and *security* are often used interchangeably. Both convey the freedom from danger, doubt, fear, and injury. But the danger or risk associated with unsafe playground equipment, or less-than-optimal adult to student ratios is not the same as the results of fighting, bullying, unsafe traffic patterns, and psychopaths who are hell bent on doing harm.

Did you ever consider the establishment of a dress code as a safety issue? Some school dress codes require that shirts be tucked in *and* all outer garments stored in lockers. This stipulation decreases the possibility of hidden weapons.

Emergency situations that require evacuating students and staff from the school campus are common occurrences. Severe weather, nearby crime, and electrical outages are among the unforeseen conditions that may require evacuation.

On one occasion, my school had an oil leak and the fumes were making some students sick. We executed our emergency evacuation plan and transferred students to a local community center or sent them home with their parents.

But, suppose the parents weren't home? If parents weren't home, or we could not contact them, we employed two safety measures that worked well. First, we had the names of people who were cleared to pick up children in case a parent couldn't. Second, we had a list of *safe houses* where kids could be dropped off until their parents or a relative could pick them up.

Today's communication devices, cell phones, computers, and texting make it infinitely easier to contact parents and caretakers. This was not the case in ancient times when I was a principal.

I briefly mentioned adult-to-student ratios as a safety consideration. School budgets are generally tight and hiring enough adults to supervise students is not usually a priority. It is a priority, however, to establish specific rules that apply to playgrounds, cafeterias, hallways, buses, and any gathering spots on campus. Once established, these rules should be in a student handbook and reviewed regularly with students. All classroom and general school rules should be sent home to parents and returned to school with their signature. This could also be an effective back-to-school-night activity.

When hundreds, and often thousands, of students assemble in one building, there are always concerns about health. Health issues cannot be taken lightly; they can yield dangerous results. Avoiding the use of toxic cleaning materials or any hazardous substances as well as providing allergy-free zones should be standard practice for today's schools.

I was always blessed with talented and caring school nurses. I relied on them daily to make appropriate decisions about a child's well-being and that of the school. They never failed me or the students. My nurses wrote and regularly distributed to parents a newsletter describing the best health practices and up-to-date health information.[1]

In light of the massacre that took place at Sandy Hook Elementary School in Newtown, Connecticut, on December 14, 2012, additional safety measures have been discussed in many schools. Your school may want to consider training staff on assessing threats, employing walking patrols every fifteen minutes, and looking out for illegally parked cars. People with evil intentions usually park near the entrance.

Equally important to note is that whatever is illegal off campus is illegal on campus. Use common sense at all times.

There is no more important issue than the safety and security of your child. Parents should be able to take comfort from knowing that their child's school is as safe and secure as possible. Accidents will happen, but they should be just that. Injuries and harm in any form should never be attributed to negligence.

An enormous amount of information regarding school safety is available through books, professional journals, government pamphlets, and the Internet. Take advantage of them. Some resources include:

- National Crime Prevention Council
- Association for Supervision and Curriculum Development
- United States Department of Education
- National Education Association

- Center for Safe Schools
- Bureau of Justice Statistics
- Local education agencies (State Department of Education)

> "Strategy is better than strength."
> —Hausa proverb

CHAPTER 4: DISCIPLINE: THE CONCEPT

"Grandfather, Sacred One, teach us love, compassion, and honor that we may heal the earth and heal each other."

—Ojibwa prayer

We all have an idea of the definition of discipline. But what does it mean specifically to you? Are your thoughts and feelings about the concept of discipline positive or negative? Consider the following terms most commonly associated with discipline: *punishment, control, management, coercion, learning, emotional intelligence, training, teaching,* and *self-restraint*. Which word or words do you feel accurately describe your concept of the idea of discipline?

The *American Heritage Dictionary* defines discipline as "training that is expected to produce a specific character or pattern of behavior, especially training that produces mental or moral improvement."

The word *training* in the above definition can be used interchangeably with the words *teaching* and *coaching*. The best way for parents, as their child's first and most influential teachers, to think about the concept of discipline is to consider it an opportunity to teach your child self-restraint and impulse control. Doing so, without resorting to coercion, bribes, rewards, or punishment, will get the best results and define you as a teacher—not a controller or manipulator.

Begin by reviewing chapter 2 and reflecting again on these three questions:

- What are your expectations for your child?
- What type of person do you hope he or she will become?
- How can you guide and help him or her to achieve this goal?

Daniel Goleman, author of the popular book *Emotional Intelligence* (1995), offers a valid starting point.

> What factors are at play, for example, when people of high IQ flounder and those of modest IQ do surprisingly well? I would argue that the difference quite often lies in the abilities called here *emotional intelligence*, which include self-control, zeal, and persistence, and the ability to motivate oneself. And these skills, as we shall see, can be taught to children, giving them a better chance to use whatever intellectual potential the genetic lottery may have given them.[1]

Goleman goes on to say that those who cannot resist acting impulsively are lacking in self-control and suffering from a "moral deficiency." He suggests two moral stances—self-restraint and compassion.[2]

We have all observed and read about the children, the adolescents, and the adults who are unable to grasp the concept of self-denial, self-sacrifice, impulse control, or compassion. The toddler screaming for a toy or treat in the supermarket, the adolescent who bullies others on the playground or experiments with alcohol, sex, or drugs, and adults who commit unspeakable crimes are examples of an inability to learn acceptable standards of behavior in a civilized society. Our detention centers, jails, and prisons are packed with people whose sense of *emotional intelligence* (self-restraint and compassion) is lost in an abyss of self-indulgence and self-gratification.

THE MARSHMALLOW TEST

How would you rate yourself on the self-control, persistence, and self-motivation meter? Do you have any self-control? Are you persistent and self-motivated? Do you desire any of these skills or are you satisfied with your current meter reading? How would your children rate on the above meter? And what difference does it make anyway?

"In studies initiated a half century ago, and still ongoing today, we've shown that this skill set is visible and measurable early in life and has profound long-term consequences for people's welfare and mental and physical health over a life span," Goleman wrote.[3]

One of the most famous studies in the field of psychology was conducted by Stanford University psychologist Walter Mischel. Between 1968 and 1974, more than 550 preschool students at Bing Nursery School in Palo Alto, California, participated in this landmark research project. The purpose of the study was to determine or understand how children develop the ability to delay gratification; considered to be a critical life skill.

The Challenge

In a room at the university's nursery school laboratory, children were offered a variety of treats ranging from marshmallows to pretzels, cookies, and mints. First the children selected the treat they wanted most and were told they could have two of those treats, "a larger reward," if they waited up to twenty minutes for the researcher to return. The researcher left the room and observed each child through a one-way glass partition.

Amy, for example, chose marshmallows. She sat alone at a table facing one marshmallow that she could have immediately, as well as the two marshmallows that she could have if she waited. Next to the treats was a desk bell she could ring at any time to call back the researcher and eat the one marshmallow. Or she could wait for the researcher to return, and if she hadn't left her chair or started to eat the marshmallow, she could have both. The struggles we observed as these children tried to restrain themselves from ringing the bell could bring tears to your eyes, have you applauding their creativeness and cheering them on, and give fresh hope for the potential of even young children to resist temptation and persevere for their delayed rewards. This project eventually turned into a longitudinal study that began when these preschoolers were four or five and followed them until they reached their late twenties and early thirties. Some were followed into their forties. What did the researchers discover?

Results

According to Mischel, the adults aged twenty-seven through thirty-two who delayed their gratification until they could eat two treats had lower body fat, a better sense of self-worth, and were goal-oriented and better at coping with stress.

But the results also raised important questions that have significant implications for raising and educating our children. Is the ability to control yourself prewired or can it be taught? What is willpower, and what are the circumstances that reduce willpower? What are the cognitive skills that produce self-control and restrain our impulses?

When I see people smoking cigarette after cigarette or filling their shopping carts with soda, snacks, and all sorts of processed food—which they also feed to their children—I am astonished at their lack of knowledge or their failure to access the current information on healthy lifestyles. I recently played golf with a guy who smoked a cigarette on each of our eighteen holes together. He told me he was seventy-five years old. Shouldn't he know better?

I must confess my own lack of self-control when it comes to chocolate. I find it hard to resist, and my willpower wilts when confronted with anything chocolate. Hey, is it my fault? Maybe I am prewired to crave this delightful treat—the fault of my mother, who also loved sweet snacks.

IMPLICATIONS FOR PARENTS

Without getting into a full-blown discussion about whether DNA or the environment has more influence on what we eventually become, suffice to say that we emerge from a not-so-easily-understandable combination of the two. This of course has enormous implications for parents motivated to become more knowledgeable and proactive as they model what they expect from their children. School and life success are nurtured at home in an environment that is characterized by tough love, compassion, sharing, kindness, and an emphasis on learning and self-improvement. Self-control is critical for future success and the attainment of long-range goals. It helps build empathy and contributes to developing lasting relationships. Instead of watching them opt for destructive behavior, we can teach our children to persevere and discipline themselves. There is always a possibility for "self-directed change."

Children who are going to succeed need parents or other significant adults, like teachers, who encourage them, believe in them, and instill an "I can do it" mindset.

There are no guarantees. Michel points out that correlations were significant for groups of children but they are not necessarily predictable for an individual child. He cites the example of heavy smokers who die of lung-related diseases, while other heavy smokers don't. My friend, a heavy smoker since his teen years, lived to a ripe old age and died of a disease unrelated to smoking.

But it's the goal that matters and "attitude" will improve your child's chances and provide the effort needed to be successful. After a concert, a fan of Itzhak Perlman, the famous violinist, rushed up to the world-renowned musician and exclaimed, "I'd give my life to play like you." Perlman calmly answered, "I did."

My parents were intelligent, hardworking, and self-sacrificing. Despite being not particularly knowledgeable about how schools function—they always sided with the teachers and the principal—their expectations were crystal clear: *We believe in you, you can do it, you are going to college. Now, get busy and take care of business.*

SUGGESTIONS FOR PARENTS

Your child's potential for success at home, in the community, and at school will be better served if you incorporate the principles of emotional intelligence into your overall pledge and the plan suggested in chapter 2. When I observe a parent at the supermarket who calmly says *no* to a relentlessly nagging toddler, I am encouraged. On occasion, I have had the opportunity to watch my daughter, Karen, interacting with my teenage granddaughter, Olivia. One day, I observed as my daughter explained—with great patience and civility, I might add—to my granddaughter why my granddaughter had to put half the money she earned at her after-school part-time job into a savings account. I am encouraged again by both my daughter's teaching moment and my granddaughter's acceptance of the logical reasons for saving some of her earnings.

When I turned sixteen and became old enough to drive, I pleaded with my father to allow me to purchase a car. Even though I had saved the money, he said no. I went behind his back and pleaded my case to my mother. It worked. My mother was a softy on that particular occasion, although in most matters she was a taskmaster and an exemplary mom who modeled life lessons and taught me well how to be responsible and selfless. Unfortunately, in this case, my parents were not presenting me with a united front, and as a teenager I used this to my advantage.

Parents have to work together and make decisions together. This will help you to avoid being manipulated by your children. Remember:

- Your pledge and your plan must include references to expected behavior, which includes self-reliance, compassion, cooperation, selflessness, and self-control.
- Learn some problem-solving techniques and conflict-resolution strategies that are void of physical, verbal, or emotional abuse, punishments, and rewards. Consequences will be necessary at times. Use moderation and common sense.
- Develop a few house rules (expected behaviors) that correlate with your goals and beliefs. State them positively, and be a living example of acceptable behavior.
- Work out your differences of opinion—do(s) and don't(s)—in private, not in front of the kids.
- Post your rules where they can be seen and referenced easily.
- The Golden Rule is always golden.
- Say often and sincerely that you believe in your child's ability to learn and succeed.

- Conduct regular family meetings in which every member has a voice—i.e., allow your children to participate in the decision-making process.

- Unacceptable behavior has consequences. When rules are broken, stand strong and be consistent. Children understand consequences. Consequences are a normal part of their actions and decision-making, whether it be at school, in sports, or in the neighborhood. Be creative, civil, and con-trolled, and avoid harshness.

- A range of opinions and innumerable books and articles are available on the topic of discipline. I recommend focus-ing on problem solving rather than punishment. I view a child's specific behavior and overall conduct as teaching opportunities. For example, a time-out for reflection and discussion and/or writing a mea culpa in a journal that can be referred to in the future may work better than a scolding or a punishment.

REWARDS

I do not believe in rewarding children for doing what should be a normal part of family life—e.g., chores, getting good grades in school, and treating family members with respect. Bribery is unacceptable. However, if you occasionally want to show your appreciation to your child for helping and being a supportive member of the family, do something special with your child or surprise him or her, but do not make it a reward. Some parents and educators believe that rewards such as stars, stickers, and pizza parties are as manipulative as punishments.

Think carefully about both rewards and consequences. If you are uncertain whether your methods are having positive or negative results, take the time to read what the experts have to say, or talk to school counselors and school psychologists. Several resources listed in the bibliography may guide your decision-making.

> "If you punish a child for being naughty, and reward him for being good, he will do right merely for the sake of the reward; and when he goes out into the world and finds out that goodness is not always rewarded, nor wickedness always punished, he will grow into a man who only thinks about how he may get on in the world, and does right or wrong according as he finds of advantage to himself."
>
> —Immanuel Kant

CHAPTER 5: DISCIPLINE IN SCHOOLS

"Fifty years ago teachers said that their top discipline problems were talking, chewing gum, making noise, and running in the halls. The current list, by contrast, sounds like a cross between a rap sheet and the seven deadly sins."

—Anna Quindlen

According to news reports, a kindergartner in Houston, Texas, brought a loaded gun to school. Apparently, the gun dropped out of his book bag in the cafeteria, went off, and injured several students.

How should the school respond? Who is responsible? Could this have been prevented?

The National Center for Education Statistics (NCES) reported that a total of 433,800 serious disciplinary actions were taken by public schools during the 2009–2010 school year. During the 2006–2007 school year, the North Carolina public school system reported that four categories of incidents were responsible for 93 percent of all reported offenses:[1]

- Possession of a controlled substance
- Possession of a weapon
- Possession of alcohol
- Assault

Reports generated at the Bureau of Justice Statistics and the NCES present startling data. Gone are the days of minor and, mostly, unreported offenses in schools. Today's "deadly sins" can and do include rape, vandalism, theft, trespassing, bomb threats, all forms of bullying, and murder.[2]

As a principal, I encouraged parents to understand how discipline works in their children's school. With this understanding, they can create a culture at home that goes hand in hand with the disciplinary environment at school.

SCHOOL CLIMATE

The starting point for a successful, positive, and safe environment is the establishment of a school climate that emphasizes kindness, gentleness, responsibility, and self-restraint. This begins with a clear and comprehensive written policy detailing expected behaviors and indicating how infractions and violations will be handled. Does your school embrace this philosophy? Find out!

With the principal's permission, and accompanied by a staff member, take a tour of your school. Observe and listen. Peek into classrooms. What do you see? Are students engaged in learning and working purposefully? When students move through the halls, are they orderly and quiet? Are verbal exchanges among teachers, students, and staff respectful? Does the building appear clean and free of obstructions and equipment? Are motivational posters and school rules clearly posted?

THE PRINCIPAL

One of the most important things parents can do is become acquainted with the principal—the school leader and primary decision maker.

Request a meeting. When I was the principal of Purchase School, I occasionally met with parents who were *thinking* of moving into our attendance area. They not only requested a meeting, but also asked for a tour of the facilities. Some of these couples had not yet started a family.

The principal's vision for school success and the ability to articulate it and carry it out will affect your child academically, socially, and emotionally. Do you trust the judgment and ability of your child's principal to lead the school and carry out its mission? Additionally, talk to other parents about their impression of the school and its leadership.

The leader of the school is visible, meaning he or she is *everywhere*: in the classrooms, the halls, the cafeteria, the library, and on the playground. During arrival and dismissal, the principal will often be seen assisting students, staff, and parents. The principal is always accessible and serves as the head cheerleader, the vision keeper, the school motto in action, the role model everyone can look up to.

Student conduct as well as student progress should be a daily topic as the principal interacts with staff, individual students, and groups of students. Does your child ever mention interacting with the principal? Has your child ever met the principal? Does the principal frequently visit classrooms?

I had the privilege of leading two elementary schools. Both of them adopted, as their school anthem, one of my favorite mottos: "Don't break any hearts." This cautionary reminder was depicted brilliantly by one of my art teachers, Laureen Grossmann, and displayed all over the school. Without fail, whenever I encountered a student in the hallway, I would always address him or her by his or her first name and ask, "Did you break any hearts today?" Of course, I always received the same reply: "No, Dr. Casale."

This may sound silly or childish to some, but the message was clear: be kind and gentle, and get along with everyone. Most did. By the time students reach the secondary level, I would suggest reminding them to think and *make good choices*. At all levels, kindness, consideration, and responsibility must rule the day, especially if we hope to live in a safer, happier world.

> "If your actions inspire others to dream more, learn more, do more, and become more, then you are a leader."
>
> —John Quincy Adams

SCHOOL DISCIPLINE PLAN

The components of a thoughtful discipline policy include:
- A goal or mission statement
- Specific belief statements
- Rules, expectations, and consequences
- Plans for communicating the policies to all stakeholders
- Evaluation and record-keeping

MISSION STATEMENTS/GOALS/BELIEFS

A goal or mission statement, as previously presented in chapter 2, is a brief and general statement of purpose. For example:

"Our mission at Carmel Elementary School is to create and foster an environment that is characterized by kindness, respect, responsibility, cooperation, compassion, good manners, self-restraint, and lifelong learning."

Specific belief statements represent clear expectations and outcomes that guide the policy and inform students, staff, and parents of the overall vision. For example:

We believe that:

1. *All students can learn how to conduct themselves in a civil manner.*
2. *All students can learn how to solve problems, conflicts, and differences without resorting to physical, verbal, nonverbal, or cyber abuse.*
3. *All parents, teachers, and staff must be part of the process that exemplifies expected norms of behavior.*
4. *The best type of discipline is self-discipline.*
5. *All students can learn how to work and play as part of a group.*

Depending upon the age group being served, the wording of the rules and expectations may differ. However it is worded, the message must be clear, brief, and stated positively. Keep the list short; brevity works best. Below are some general school rules that apply to all levels:

- Follow directions.
- Make good choices.
- Respect people and property.
- Say and do kind things.
- Do no harm.
- Think before you act.

Consequences will also differ according to the age group being served. General consequences at all levels may include referrals, parent contact, counseling, detention, loss of privileges, suspensions, alternative placement, student courts and mediation, and the inclusion of law enforcement. My recommendations are to follow district and school policies. Be consistent and creative, and use common sense.

The dissemination-and-communication component of any policy is critical. A document that sits on the shelf and collects dust is a waste of valuable time and effort and will never impact your school. To have a positive and lasting impact, the school leader must make the policy a priority, and the staff must believe in it and invest themselves in its success.

Many schools distribute handbooks full of policies, rules, and guidelines. Expectations should be front and center at the beginning of the handbook. Some schools require parents and students to sign an acknowledgment that they not only have read the discipline portion of the policy, but understand it as well.

Conduct should be a daily topic in each classroom. The principal's role has already been described in this chapter, but the daily contact that teachers have with students presents the best opportunity to revisit expectations for behavior on a consistent basis.

Evaluation and record-keeping drive the success of the discipline plan. Careful record-keeping will determine the number of referrals and types of negative behavior that occur. This documentation will provide input to the ongoing committee—composed of staff and parents—and will facilitate decision making that will guide the entire process of establishing a safer and more secure environment for students and staff.

All parents should be confident their children are learning in a safe and secure environment, but parents must also understand that their cooperation, vigilance, and participation are needed to achieve desired outcomes. Working parents may not be able to volunteer or serve on committees, but they can review disciplinary policies with their children and conduct discussions about proper conduct as part of their daily conversations. I suggest incorporating aspects of the school policy into family policy. If concerns arise, ask questions, become knowledgeable and be a part of the solution.

"It takes less time to do a thing right than to explain why you did it wrong."

—Henry Wadsworth Longfellow

CHAPTER 6: BULLYING

"Our deeds determine us, as much as we determine our deeds."

—George Eliot, *Adam Bede*

Bullying, in all its many forms, is pervasive in our schools at every level—elementary school, middle school, high school, and college. Obviously, physical, emotional, and verbal abuse must be curtailed. Yet current statistics are alarming, and, although schools are engaged in a variety of anti-bullying efforts, problems persist and positive results are uneven. Parents must become a part of those efforts. They must be a part of the solution.

In May 2012, the parents of an eighth-grade boy in a private Christian school in Florida sued the school, claiming that another student had kicked and stabbed their son with pencils. Lawyers for the victim stated that his injuries twice required a trip to the emergency room. Private schools are not immune to this epidemic. Paul Coughlin, an expert and author of numerous books on bullying, has been quoted as saying, "No school is immune to bullying."

In 2011, a fight in a Palm Beach County, Florida, middle school was recorded on a camera phone and later broadcast on local TV and YouTube. Of all the details reported, two are especially noteworthy:

- The principal of the school was quoted as saying, "This goes on in many other local middle schools."

- District policy does not permit fighting back. It does permit the victim to ward off the bully's punches. Both boys were suspended.[1]

"I'm a monster!" Those are the words Wayne Treacy, a ninth grader from Deerfield Beach, Florida, used at his arrest for repeatedly stomping with steel-toed boots on the head of Josie Lou Ratley. This gruesome act, which left Ratley with permanent nerve damage, was the result of a sarcastic text message Ratley sent to Treacy regarding Treacy's brother's recent suicide.[2]

Other recent examples of extreme bullying include:

- Terrifying attacks at Columbine High School in Colorado (1999), where students and staff were murdered by two student shooters who had reportedly been victims of bullying
- Increased adolescent suicides due to bullying and cyberbullying
- A hazing incident at Florida A&M University in 2012 that resulted in the death of a band member

THE DATA

Major findings from the 2009 Crime Supplement to the National Crime Victimization Survey reveal that approximately 28 percent of students ages twelve to seventeen have been bullied at school. In 2009, the Centers for Disease Control and Prevention published a bullying report based on a survey of nearly six thousand public, middle-, and high-school students in Massachusetts, entitled the "Youth Risk Behavior Survey."[3]

The report indicated that 43.9 percent of middle-school students were affected by bullying. In high school, the number dropped to 30.5

percent. These figures are accurate only to the extent that they were reported by students and recorded by the schools surveyed. The study also revealed what researchers have known for a long time: bullying is linked to risk factors such as poor grades, drug use, alcohol use, and family violence.

Additional data are available through numerous sources, including the National Education Association and the United States Justice Department. The Justice Department's guide on bullying, issued through the office of Community Oriented Policing Services, states that bullying is the most underreported problem in American schools.[4]

DEFINING BULLYING

If you were to make a list of the behaviors that define bullying, what would it include? Would fighting, pushing, shoving, name-calling, insulting, and taunting be among the infractions you listed? Those are the most common manifestations of bullying, but are you aware that any type of physical or verbal harassment that is intended to harm someone is considered bullying? With that in mind, your list needs to be expanded to include stalking, threatening, taking someone's property, and, according to author Kathleen Winkler in her book on *Bullying* (2005), causing someone to be "socially isolated by excluding her or him" from a group.[5]

Cyberbullying

Jamey Rodemeyer, a fourteen-year-old boy from Buffalo, New York, committed suicide after he was bullied about his sexuality via the Internet. Some of the messages Jamey received were intentionally vicious, including, "I wouldn't care if you died. So just do it."

Jennifer Holladay, former director of teaching tolerance at the Southern Poverty Law Center, defines cyberbullying as the use of technology to harass, humiliate, and/or threaten.[6] Social-networking sites, such as Facebook and Twitter, along with texting and emails, have successfully combined to establish a technology system that encourages bullying.

During my childhood in ancient times, passing notes around the classroom mocking someone else was the height of nonconfrontational bullying. If the teacher intercepted the note, he or she acted quickly by confronting the note bully, issuing a warning, sending the student to the office, or all three. This is no longer the case. Modern technology allows thousands of viewers to access and surreptitiously join the attacks.

It doesn't appear that today's electronic communication technology, which many kids—including my grandchildren—are addicted to, will be disappearing any time soon. Imagine the consternation, the dismay, and the horror if parents told their children they had to give up their mobile phones, computers, and other handheld devices. The results would be protests, riots, and a march on Washington.

Give up texting? Give up my online activity?! I would prefer to give up candy, ice cream, and going to the mall. I would rather make my bed and do the dishes than be without my electronic devices.

But what if a bully started stalking your child online? This is what cyberbullies do. They attack from a distance by saying mean or harsh things; they spread rumors and hide their identity. Some cyberbullies tell their friends to email or post hurtful messages. The Centers for Disease Control and Prevention identified cyberbullying as an emerging health problem, and researchers report that one third of all teens who use the Internet have been cyberbullied.

Let's be realistic. Parents are not routinely going to take away cell phones and computers, though it remains an option. For practical reasons, cell phones provide the contact with children that most parents find indispensable, and computers—when used for educational purposes—are a valuable tool for school and life success. But, if knowledge is power, it is incumbent upon parents to be as savvy as possible about the dangers lurking in the form of electronics abuse. It is the supreme responsibility of parents to protect their children from any physical, emotional, or psychological danger. If you suspect bullying, look for changes in behavior such as anxiety and depression. A child not wanting to go to school or quitting a school club or sport could also be a sign of behavioral change.

SEXTING: IT'S A FELONY

A speaker at a school assembly asked his audience to shut their eyes, put their heads down, and raise their hands if the answer to the following question was yes: "Did you ever send or receive a naked picture of someone sixteen years old or younger?"

Approximately fifty hands were raised. The guest speaker then informed his audience that those who raised their hands had broken the law.

The speaker was Gregory Schiller, the Assistant State Attorney for the state of Florida. His audience—including teachers who also had to comply with the directive to shut their eyes and put their heads down—was comprised of the eighth-grade students at Watson B. Duncan Middle School in Palm Beach Gardens, Florida.

There was stunned silence among those who had raised their hands.

Gregory Schiller has spent the past few years traveling around the state and speaking to teens, parents, and school officials about the danger of online predators who send naked and explicit photos through cell phones or online.

Schiller, who has prosecuted hundreds of Internet offenders, told his audience that sexting has become a *silent epidemic* and explained why those who raised their hands were guilty of committing a felony. "It is illegal to send or receive naked photos of underage children even if the sender or receiver is also underage."

Students were then asked to consider the following scenario: A young girl sends a naked picture of herself to her boyfriend. The boyfriend might then share that picture with his friends, who in turn send it to their friends. It could also eventually be viewed by online predators. So what the sender thinks is private, between herself and her boyfriend, isn't.

It is emphasized in this report that Schiller uses the word *sexting* only with eighth graders who will soon be in high school. He does *not* use the word *sex* when he is talking to grade levels below the eighth grade.

PROTECTING YOUR CHILD

My message to parents is consistent: become knowledgeable and proactive in your child's education both in and out of school. Do you know whether your child is active on social media? Half the children who have heard Mr. Schiller's presentations were active on Facebook before they were thirteen years old. Many also had Twitter accounts and most also had Instagram accounts. In other words, be smart and be vigilant about social media. These suggestions from the FBI are worth noting:

- Keep computers and other electronics out of children's bedrooms and in a public place in the house.
- All electronics are turned off at a stated hour (say, 8:00 p.m.) and plugged in to a family recharge station. Parents, too.
- Turn wireless Internet signals off at a designated time.

- Opt for flip phones instead of smart phones that provide Internet services. (Remember the days when the reason for supplying your child with a phone was for the sole purpose of your son or daughter maintaining contact with you and *not* the rest of the world?)
- Talk to your child about victimization and the potential for online danger.
- Spend time with your children online and let them teach you about their favorite web destinations.
- Use parental controls from your service provider. Chat rooms must be monitored.
- Maintain access to your child's online accounts, check email, and be up front about why this is necessary.
- Know what computer safeguards your child's school has in place, as well as those in the local library and in the homes of your child's friends.

The FBI advises that children never:

- Arrange a face-to-face meeting with someone they meet online
- Upload pictures of themselves to people they do not know
- Give out identifying information
- Download pictures from an unknown source
- Respond to messages or bulletin board postings that are suggestive, obscene, belligerent or harassing

PARENTAL RESPONSIBILITY

Simply knowing that cyberbullies are out there intending to do harm is your first line of defense. This is linked to knowing what your children are doing on their cell phones and computers. Second, make time for family discussions. Turn off the TV, limit electronic use to specific times, and talk to your children during uninterrupted periods about school, their friends, and bullies, including cyberbullies. Kids need to know they can talk to you. Hey, how about this novel idea? Get a book from the library on cyberbullying and read it together as a family.

Please understand that most children usually lack the maturity to understand the consequences of their actions on these devices you so generously provided them. Adolescents should be taught to be leaders not followers, especially when it comes to attacking another child. Unfortunately, kids fall prey to the "groupthink" mentality and follow the crowd for fear of being isolated.

Parents are the first and primary transmitters of the family culture. Imagine how few bullies there would be if parents were teaching and modeling kindness, compassion, and empathy. Consider electronic devices as parenting tools and not a gift or a license to exceed the boundaries of respect and good taste.

Any harsh words, rumors, or threats directed at your child, including embarrassing photos (sexting), are all forms of cyberbullying. On the other hand, if your child ever forwarded a message or photo that was hurtful or demeaning to someone else, they would be guilty of cyberbullying, even if the message or photo didn't originate with him or her. All of this is worth talking about.

Thirdly, even if your child has been taught not to accept or forward mean-spirited messages or rumors, there is more that can be done to halt the madness. If the cyberbully's identity is known, talk to him and his parents. Make sure you have reliable proof by saving texts and emails. Express your displeasure in a civil tone; state the facts as well as the unfortunate consequences that befall the victims of cyberbullying: depression, anxiety and fear, even suicide in some cases. Remain active and alert.

Parents can exercise their parental authority by blocking websites, receiving alerts when their kids search for them, and by recording their phone activity. Software such as Mobile Spy enables parents to see all text messages. You are *not* a spy. You're the parent, the teacher, and the role model . . . and you have a right to know.

Finally, collaborate with the school. A cyberbully seeks power and is no one's real friend. The bully often suffers from emotional and behavioral issues that he can also inflict on his victims. Schools have rules against bullying and cyberbullying. Unfortunately, courts have sent mixed and vague messages on the issue. But while free speech is protected, harassing speech is not. "Schools should connect their discipline codes to civil rights laws," according to Wendy J. Murphy, adjunct professor at the New England School of Law.

> "You must be the change you wish to see in the world."
> —Mahatma Gandhi

THE MYTHS ABOUT BULLYING

In *Dealing with Bullying in Schools* (2004), authors Mona O'Moore and Stephen Minton reveal six standard myths about bullying:

- It's part of life.
- Boys will be boys.
- It happens at all schools; don't worry.
- Sticks and stones will break my bones, but words will never harm me.
- Bullying never did me any harm.

- It'll toughen you up.[7]

These statements, of course, are worse than myths—they're nonsense! Bullying is not part of life and is not acceptable in any way or under any circumstances. Bullying will not toughen a child up.

THE SCHOOL'S RESPONSE

In their book, *And Words Can Hurt Forever* (2002), authors James Garbarino and Ellen deLara write:

"What do we learn from listening to kids talk about school safety? We learn that even in schools that adults consider physically safe, many children feel threatened."[8]

The authors go on to say that "the system and culture of the school is responsible for continuing harassment and emotional violence."[9]

Many schools across the country have taken up the challenge of confronting and reducing the incidences of bullying. Those measures include:

- Adopting anti-bullying programs
- Blanketing the school with posters and slogans
- Giving out anti-bullying T-shirts
- Offering conflict-resolution lessons as part of the curriculum
- Hosting guest speakers on the topic
- Providing in-service training to all staff
- Monitoring *hot spots* around the school—e.g., hallways, cafeteria, playground, parking lots, and buses—with appropriate student/teacher ratios
- Distributing policy statements to students and parents that require acknowledgment and signatures

- Seeking parent involvement on committees
- Conducting parent meetings to discuss policies
- Utilizing student and parent surveys to gather data
- Documenting reported incidents
- Consistently following up on consequences
- Providing counseling support
- Reviewing, evaluating, and adjusting school policies on a regular basis

All of the above are admirable—yet worthless unless the school has the dedicated leadership required to effect change. I have known some principals who could not lead a line of fourth graders to a water fountain without incident. I have also known principals and their assistants who could well have been invisible, so rarely were they seen around their school. But I have also know principals whose dedication and devotion to students, parents, and staff knew no bounds as they strove to create a safer and more secure learning environment. The truth remains that, in our less-than-perfect world, no one is going to care more about a child than his or her most important teachers, nurturers, and protectors—parents.

SUGGESTIONS FOR PARENTS

Parents must make it their priority to be knowledgeable about all school policies, initiatives, and efforts. Do not wait for the school to inform you. You could be waiting a long time. Be proactive. Ask questions and request the information you want. In my experience, schools offer information to parents on a need-to-know basis or in times of crisis.

If a school is to be safe, parents must be committed to involving themselves in the process. Accidents will happen even under the best of circumstances, and, realistically speaking, bullying will never be eradicated entirely. However, negligence should never be part of the equation. The following suggestions will assist parents in making informed decisions both at home and at school:

- Educate yourself about legislation passed in your state regarding bullying and cyberbullying.
- Determine whether the legislation is part of your school district's policy.
- Become more informed about bullying. Access books, journal articles, videos and websites. (I encourage parents and teachers to view the award-winning documentary *Bully* by Lee Hirsch. It chronicles the experiences of several students who suffered as a result of bullying in their respective schools. *Time* magazine movie reviewer Richard Corliss called it "the movie your kids must see." Urge your parent organization to view it in parts across several meetings. Use it as an opportunity to discuss and fine-tune what is going on at your school to combat endemic concern. Learn more at the bullyproject.com where you will find tools and resources to put the brakes on bullying.)
- If you have the time, serve on school discipline committees.
- Advise your child, who may be a victim or a bystander, to report incidences of bullying. Find out if your school has a policy whereby the reporter (bystander) remains unidentified.
- Model your expectations by learning and using conflict-resolution strategies at home.
- Along with other like-minded parents, form a group and work cooperatively with school officials.

- Limit cell phone ownership and use by age and level of maturity. For most students under the age of sixteen, cell phones, if provided, should be programmed for emergency purposes and family interaction.
- Limit and monitor social networking and email accounts. Better yet, avoid social networks altogether.
- If your child is involved in a bullying incident at school, arrange an immediate conference with the teacher or the supervising adult.
- Do not rule out notifying law enforcement officials for serious offenses.
- If all other options fail, withdraw from the school and seek a safer environment.
- Seek the involvement of the school's parent organization.
- Become acquainted with all your child's friends and their parents.
- Insist on more face-to-face interactions and play dates for your younger children.

Remain vigilant, proactive, and knowledgeable. Ask questions. There is nothing more important than your child's safety. Talk daily with your children about the entire school day—arrival to dismissal. Your family goal and mission statement will guide your plan of action.

> "For of all sad words of tongue or pen,
> The saddest are these: 'It might have been!'"
> —John Greenleaf Whittier

CHAPTER 7: HIGHLY EFFECTIVE TEACHERS

"It is the supreme art of the teacher to awaken joy in creative expression and knowledge."

—Albert Einstein

The teacher as artist: Have you ever experienced one? Known one? Seen one? They are the gold medalists of the education profession. Highly effective teachers, in my opinion, rank above the great actors, writers, poets, singers, dancers, artists, sculptors, and gifted athletes that our popular culture admires. The artistry and talent of highly effective teachers is never one-dimensional. They don't mold clay; they mold minds. The great ones don't just make students think; they change habits and shape attitudes. While highly effective teachers may bring an element of entertainment to their lessons, it's not their sole purpose. Inspiring students to become lifelong learners is their goal. The best of them leave legacies beyond the classroom.

Money, rewards, and recognition are not what draw these dedicated professionals to the field of education. Teachers know from the outset that it's not about them—it's about their students. The great teachers are devoted and dedicated to their art. They are devoid of ego, always selfless. Teachers function in loco parentis—in place of parents. Their devotion knows no bounds as they fiercely protect their students from harm. They would give their lives for their students—and they did at Sandy Hook Elementary School in Newtown, Connecticut.

In 2012, the popular website www.studentsfirst.org conducted a contest in which participants were asked to describe their favorite teacher in six words. One of the entries was "I'll remember her in 50 years."[1] Do you remember your favorite teacher and the impact she or he had on you? I'll bet you do, and no matter how many years have passed, that person's methods, caring, and influence remain with you even today.

> "The greatest use of a life is to spend it for something that will outlast it."
>
> —Ralph Waldo Emerson

THE EFFECTIVE TEACHER PARADIGM

Our favorite teachers inspire us to try harder, do better, and accomplish more than we think we can. The only other person with that much influence is a parent. Here's how to recognize superior teachers in your own life and your child's life:

- You wanted to be in their class.
- You wanted to please them.
- You wanted to do their homework.
- You wanted their attention.
- You worked hard for them.
- You were never bored.
- They treated you respectfully and fairly.
- They were knowledgeable.
- They knew how to explain things.
- They made you feel special.
- They inspired you.

- They made learning fun, useful, and relevant.
- They were enthusiastic and positive.
- They organized lots of activities that permitted talking, listening to each other, moving around, and handling materials.
- They left you feeling prepared for the next grade.
- They taught you how to get along with everyone in your class.
- They were excellent role models.

Based on the above criteria, how many highly effective teachers have you encountered beginning in kindergarten and progressing through the remainder of your formal education? My unscientific surveys always reveal a number below seven. One of the main reasons for our failing schools and the mediocre education they deliver is a paucity of outstanding educators. In an interview about his book *Class Warfare: Inside the Fight to Fix America's Schools*, author-lawyer Steven Brill remarked, "Heroic educators can change kid's lives—but there will never be enough of them."

Since there are not enough outstanding teachers, parents must become more informed and take a proactive stance on behalf of their child's education. The chances for school reform and student success increase when parents fully participate.

It is imperative that you do not assess a teacher on merely personal characteristics. Being pleasant, cordial, mannerly, respectful, or just plain nice are all good qualities, but they do not necessarily translate into being top-notch teachers. Be sure that a teacher's credentials, qualifications, and experience are appropriate to his or her assigned grade level and subject. Elementary teachers are generalists who teach more than one subject but must be licensed and certified.

Secondary teachers and specific-subject teachers, such as reading specialists, must have a degree in their specialty and must be licensed and certified.

Do not hesitate to ask about credentials, qualifications, and experience, bearing in mind that even the most experienced and qualified teachers do not necessarily guarantee that your child is entering the realm of a true artist. In recent years, great emphasis has been placed on class size. Do *not* obsess over the number of students in any one class. Arne Duncan, US Secretary of Education, believes—and rightly so, in my opinion—that most parents would rather see their child in a class of thirty students with an outstanding teacher than in a class of twenty-five students with an average teacher.[2]

While parents are not professionally qualified to evaluate their child's teacher, a basic knowledge of effective teaching will be helpful in formulating opinions. The more knowledge parents have at their disposal, the more effective they will be in discussing their child's performance with teachers and administrators. There are some common criteria.

Highly effective teachers:

- Really like kids
- Are passionate about teaching and learning
- Are always prepared and organized
- Fill their classrooms with a variety of books and other exciting learning materials
- Maintain regular contact with parents
- Work closely with parents and school personnel, viewing them as resources that enhance instruction
- Are reflective about their work and always want to perform better

- Organize their classroom for activity, interaction, and engagement
- Have few or no discipline problems
- Provide instruction that is linked to state standards, benchmarks, and curricula
- Use interdisciplinary approaches that integrate subject matter. For example, a social studies unit would incorporate language arts and possibly science, math, art, and music.
- Capitalize on and use students' strengths and interests
- Assess students in a variety of ways that include portfolios, performance tasks, projects, journals, reports, and demonstrations
- Vary instruction to address various learning styles. Incorporate auditory, visual, movement, and hands-on activities into lessons
- Use technology wisely
- Infuse lessons with critical-thinking skills, problem solving, and risk taking
- Maintain and communicate high and clear expectations
- Are good at explaining things
- Know their subject
- Are enthusiastic and have a sense of humor
- Are open-minded and accept suggestions from students, colleagues, and parents
- Strike that delicate balance between fun and interesting and businesslike and productive
- Are under control at all times
- Seek learning opportunities to become better at their job
- Provide work that extends and challenges

- Design lessons that are relevant and use current events to teach required skills and concepts

Though the above list is not totally comprehensive, and not in any particular order, it should help you to determine whether the learning environment in your child's classroom is superior, average, or below average.

To take a more active role in assessing your child's teacher:

- Communicate often with the teacher by email or phone. Schedule a conference, if necessary, if you have questions or experience problems. Be prepared to ask questions about curriculum, instruction, classroom management, discipline, or anything else that concerns you. Public school teachers are government employees—they work for you. Respect their advice.

- Maintain a portfolio of your child's work. Begin in kindergarten and continue throughout the school years (K–12). Use examples of your child's work to monitor progress and obtain information that will be useful for discussions with teachers and other school personnel.

- Maintain a copy of the school curriculum in your home and familiarize yourself with it. It describes what your child is supposed to know and be able to do. Discuss the curriculum with your child to determine whether he or she understands what is expected. This document is the framework for creating learning activities. If you have questions or require explanations, meet with the teacher.

- Expect to see student assignments that challenge your child. If all you see are traditional worksheets, workbooks, and assignments that the whole class is doing, be assured that your child's imagination is not being stretched.

- Observe a lesson in the classroom.
- Talk to your child daily about the work he or she is doing. Does he or she understand it? Is he or she working hard enough?

It is important to get to know your child's teacher(s). Meetings are the best option. Informed, concerned, and involved parents experience a level of satisfaction that other parents do not share. Competent and open-minded teachers will not just listen to concerns and suggestions; they will act on them.

> "Gentlemen, we are going to relentlessly chase perfection, knowing full well we will not catch it, because nothing is perfect. But we are going to relentlessly chase it, because in the process we will catch excellence. I am not remotely interested in just being good."
> —Vince Lombardi, coach of the Green Bay Packers

"From a child I was fond of reading, and all the little money that came into my hands was ever laid out in books."

—Benjamin Franklin

Did you know that Benjamin Franklin was the most celebrated, talked-about, and revered scientist of his time in both America and Europe? He was at the top of his class at Boston Latin School and was preparing to attend Harvard University, now the oldest institution of learning in the United States. However, as he was the tenth child among seventeen siblings and the youngest son, his father considered the expense too burdensome.

Although he did not receive a formal education, Franklin became a leading diplomat, inventor, business strategist, and writer. His extraordinary and remarkable life began with an insatiable curiosity and a love of books and reading. Franklin founded the first American library in his beloved Philadelphia.

Many of our Founding Fathers were also voracious readers and accomplished writers. John Adams and Thomas Jefferson admired Franklin and sought his advice. These men were known to study and read the classics. Thomas Jefferson had the largest private library in North America. Reportedly, there were more than ten thousand books in his collection.

READING AS A FOUNDATION

Reading ranks the highest on the learning ladder because all other learning proceeds from this critical skill. Your child's chances for success and the fulfillment of his potential increase greatly if he takes this task seriously and masters learning to read.

> "Reading maketh the full man, conference a ready man, and writing an exact man."
>
> —Sir Francis Bacon

Reading is defined as the "process of constructing meaning from text."[1] Decoding words (knowing the sound that each syllable makes) and pronouncing them correctly is not reading. I once had a brilliant kindergartner who could read the *Wall Street Journal*. Her abilities at that age were impressive, but she wasn't really reading, because she did not comprehend the meaning of the words that she was able to say.

The ultimate goal is not simply to master the ability to read and comprehend; it is to learn to think. Educator and researcher Robert Marzano points this out in the curriculum-development book *Dimensions of Thinking*: "Certainly the success of any democratic system depends on individuals' ability to analyze problems and make thoughtful decisions."[2]

I will add that your child's future success in any endeavor will require the ability not to merely analyze problems but to solve problems and evaluate issues and situations. Failure to master the ability to read and think has long-term negative consequences that affect a child's self-confidence, motivation, and potential.

Create a learning culture in your home that emphasizes reading. You don't need to be a Rhodes Scholar. You do need basic knowledge, perseverance, and a commitment to your plan. You also need to set an example for your children by adhering to the "do as I do" philosophy. In an article for the *Harvard Business Review*, professor Clayton Christensen suggested, "Families have cultures just as companies do."[3] What this means is that parents are capable of establishing a literate environment in their home.

It was recently reported that 40 percent of the high school graduates in Florida are inadequately prepared for college and subsequently must take remedial reading, English, and math classes to prepare for the college curriculum. It's never too late to learn to read and think, but this is a relevant example of "the earlier, the better." A love of reading starts with you, the parent. Fill your house with good books, set an example by demonstrating your own reading habits, and joyously read those bedtime stories to your children. One caveat: you can't make your children read any more than you can make them eat peas or listen to opera, but you can set the table and you can cultivate the soil.

FILL YOUR HOUSE WITH GOOD BOOKS

> "The man who doesn't read good books has no advantage over the man who can't read."
>
> —Mark Twain

Request the Newbery Medal- and Caldecott Medal-winning books from your school's media specialist or the public librarian. These are children's and young adult titles that have received national awards for excellence in writing and illustration. Elicit advice about reading material that matches your child's grade level and interest. If your child is interested in specific topics, such as sports, nature, animals, or planes, start with those topics. Buy subscriptions to magazines that are age- and interest-appropriate, such as *Highlights* and *Sports Illustrated for Kids*. Get creative.

When I teach reading to college freshmen who did not pass the college entrance exam, I recognize that motivation is essential to success. Knowing that, I use anything that I think will arouse their interest and keep them focused.

Many of my students arrive early and spend their time before class staring at the ceiling or playing with their cell phones. Though I used to be frustrated at the sight of wasting time, it stirred my creative juices. I decided to bring a variety of shopping catalogs to class (Lands' End, Sears, Brookstone, and Hammacher Schlemmer, to name a few) and directed them to find something they wanted to order. Then I asked them to read the descriptions of their order and explain why they wanted to purchase that particular item. The smiles on their faces and their active participation revealed that this assignment was fun. It worked! I enjoyed the same success with young adults in my ESL (English as a second language) class when I used their favorite song lyrics to teach English.

ESTABLISHING ROUTINES

Schedule a regular, quiet time on all school nights for reading and/or homework. Set up a noise-free zone, a place void of any distractions. If a homework assignment includes reading (it always should), your child should fulfill the reading requirement first, because of the amount of concentration it calls for. The ultimate goal, regardless of grade level, is to continually improve reading skills that range from simple comprehension to analysis and evaluation.

If time and energy permit, read age-appropriate books of interest aloud to younger children. Read the book on your own before sharing it with your child. Seek recommendations from librarians, media specialists, and teachers. When you finish sharing the book, talk about it. Ask simple questions about the content and the characters, and encourage your child to share her comments and opinions.

Be mindful that the language arts curriculum taught in school consists of more than just reading. Writing, speaking, and listening are also components of this critical subject and are essential to communication. Except for writing, you can begin to model and expose these important language components to your infants and toddlers if you choose to read to them regularly. Encourage older siblings to read to their younger brothers and sisters. These are wonderful bonding opportunities.

READ ALOUD

Make a point to read aloud to your infants, toddlers, preschoolers, and primary grade children. Holding your baby in your lap, your toddler snuggled next to you on the couch, and that little cherub dozing off in bed while you read a favorite bedtime story are memorable events that your kids will remember and cherish. And eventually they will carry on this tradition when they become parents. Thanks, Mom. Thanks, Dad.

Embrace a variety of genres in fiction and nonfiction: picture books; biographies of heroes, presidents, and scientists; fantasy; sports; animals; space adventures; fairy tales; and poetry. Your choices are unlimited: "so many books; so little time." Seek recommendations from the school and public librarian. Buy your child's favorite books and start their bedroom library before they can read.

Make the effort to get your kids hooked on reading but don't force feed them. Sometimes a series will pique their interest: *Ivy the*

Bean and *Judy Moody* for beginning readers, the *Harry Potter* and *Percy Jackson* series for grades 3-5. My grandsons have varied interests and are voracious readers. Christian, age 16, loves history and military books; Charlie, age 14, devours books about nature, animals, and anything science-related; Kieran and Luca love sports books. Bottom line: they're reading. Kids go through phases. Stay alert to their interests.

YOUR CHILD'S FAVORITE AUTHOR

In the mid-1980s, when I was the principal of Purchase School in Harrison, New York, the faculty and I decided to switch from basal readers (books with boring and abridged reading selections) to a whole-language program which emphasized the interrelatedness of the language arts—reading, writing, speaking, and listening. The key component of this program was the emphasis on reading entire books as opposed to reading excerpts of books. Beginning in kindergarten, every grade level was assigned a list of books that teachers could choose from. Those books would become the core of that grade level's language arts program, and children would not only learn to read, but also write and speak and listen.

After a short time in the program, our students were reading a variety of books, and becoming acquainted with specific authors. One morning during my regular rounds of visiting classrooms, I quietly eased into a first grade classroom and sat in an empty chair next to Monica. The conversation follows:

Me: "Hi Monica, how are you today?"
Monica: "Fine, Dr. Casale."
Me: "Do you like school?"

Monica: "Yes, it's fun."

Me: "Do you like your teacher?"

Monica: "Yes, very much. She is so nice."

Me: "What are you reading?"

Monica: "*Where the Wild Things Are.*"

Me: "Do you have a favorite author?"

Monica: "I like this book very much, but my favorite author is Tomie dePaolo."

Me: "Which book of his did you like best?"

Monica: "*Strega Nona.* I read it five times."

I was stunned that a first grader had a favorite author. When I was in first grade, I don't think I knew the meaning of the word *author*. On other occasions while visiting classrooms, I asked the teacher if I could address the class and ask the same question of the entire class. Hands shot up like loose helium balloons. Most kids had a definitive answer. This—acquiring favorite books and favorite authors—is what all kids should experience in school and at home.

CALDECOTT AND NEWBERY AWARDS

The Caldecott Medal books honor the nineteenth-century English illustrator Randolph Caldecott. Each year the Association for Library Services for Children, a division of the American Library Association, selects "the most distinguished American picture book for children." In 2014, the award went to Brian Floca for his book, *Locomotive*.

The Newbery Medal is named in honor of the eighteenth-century London bookseller—the first publisher of children's books—John Newbery. This medal represents the "most distinguished contribution to American literature for children." Kate DiMillo was the winner in

2014 for her book, *Flora & Ulysses: The Illuminated Adventures*. Both categories also award honorable mention medals.

Your public library and your school library will have lists of Caldecott and Newbery winners. The one I have includes all the winners from 1980 to the present. Obtain a copy or download a copy from your computer and keep it handy in your home.

Join the library before your child is born. Be on a first-name basis with your librarians. Fill your house with good books and model, encourage, and inspire your child to read, read, and read some more.

DON'T FORGET THE CLASSICS

Classic books become classics because they engage generation after generation in pleasurable reading. The works of Dr. Seuss, *Charlotte's Web*, *Charlie and the Chocolate Factory*, *Treasure Island*, *Little House on the Prairie*, and many more, are books your children will hand down to their children.

E-READERS

I am not a fan of electronics unless they are used for educational purposes. E-readers, to this septuagenarian, will never replace my page-turner books, but they do have a place in our reading hierarchy. They are especially useful for kids and adults while on vacation or on long car trips. They replace bulky books and save on gas mileage. (I made that up.)

Do you have to read the same storybook over and over? Yes, if your child wants to hear it over and over. Repetitive language, vocabulary, rhythm, and the pleasure your child derives from the experience are all positives. Consider the following conversation in the cartoon *For Better or For Worse*, by Lynn Johnston:

Lizzie (pushing the book in Dad's face): *"Ding Dong Ducky?!"*

Dad: "Not again, Lizzie. I've read you this story a hundred times!"

Dad: "If I read this again, I am going to go stark raving mad!!

Dad: "You don't want your old dad to turn into a screaming weirdo, do you?

Dad: "Ding Dong Ducky was a happy little ducky . . ."[4]

If you meet resistance on the reading front, be patient. Stick to your plan, which includes filling your house with a variety of appealing reading materials. Remind your child, if necessary, why reading is important, and link it to future success and fulfillment. Model, model, model!

SOME THOUGHTS ON HOMEWORK

Homework guidelines vary considerably from school district to school district. As a school principal, I have fielded complaints from parents about too much homework, too little homework, and homework that appears to be just busy work. If you have any of these concerns, speak to your child's teacher or, if necessary, an administrator.

How do you feel about the topic of homework? Some schools have banned it because it takes the joy out of learning. These schools allow students to make decisions about what they want to take home and do for homework. Music practice, science projects, and journal writing are most popular.

Homework remains a controversial subject, as many question the value of extending the school day with what appear to be boring, confusing, repetitive, and mindless assignments. The prolific author and lecturer Alfie Kohn suggests that homework is all pain and no gain and advises that there is no definitive link between homework and student achievement.[5]

Never—not under any circumstances, and regardless of your personal beliefs about homework—do your child's homework. Establish school-night routines—a time and a place devoid of distractions—and be available for moral support and assurance that assignments were completed. This is an opportune time to catch up on your reading.

JOURNAL WRITING

It is widely accepted that proficient readers are not necessarily proficient writers, but the converse is usually true. Proficient writers are almost always skilled readers. Writing requires precision, clarity, thoughtfulness, and creativity. Writing is a critical skill. Journal writing can be a pleasurable project for the entire family. This is not to be confused with keeping a diary, which is meant to be personal and private. Journal writing is a commentary on the day's events, experiences, thoughts, and recollections that are as enjoyable in the retelling as in the writing.

My friend Mary Cunningham maintains a book journal. She records the title and author of each book she reads. She also adds a brief synopsis and her opinion of the book. When she recommends a book to a friend, she shares this information as well.

Journals can be used for recording memories of vacations, family gatherings, parties, school events, and trips. Journals can also offer feedback on entertainment such as movies, plays, and concerts, as well as impressions of new friends. (Or similar) Basically, any and all activities—the expected and the unexpected—are rich sources for journal entries. Writing translates into more reading opportunities, and thus more learning and more thinking.

A LIBRARY FOR ALL SEASONS

Libraries never skip a season and offer year-round activities and resources to accommodate each family member's interest and joy. Grab your library cards and make regular weekly scheduled visits. Make it a fun event—something the family looks forward to.

Libraries are no longer just book depositories. They serve the community by providing computer access, CDs, DVDs, recorded books, newspapers, research opportunities, and a wide variety of literacy activities and instructional forums, such as lectures. Librarians are knowledgeable and helpful, and, best of all, libraries are free.

Let the children choose a movie that the whole family can watch. Plan a visit to a zoo, an aquarium, or a farm, but go to the library first and choose books relevant to what you expect to see. Read them with the family before you go.

LIMITING TELEVISION

Television is the Looney Tunes tube. It's a thief that steals precious time from our children, when they could be doing something useful and fulfilling, like expanding their minds instead of depleting their brain cells. How about playing outside, which is fun and provides much-needed exercise? Or digging out a board game the whole family can get involved in?

Studies indicate that academic achievement drops sharply for children who watch too much TV. I am not suggesting that parents eliminate television completely, but I do recommend that viewing time be limited and supervised. Televisions should not be allowed in children's bedrooms.

Limited television viewing does not apply to programs that are educational and that may provide opportunities for Mom and Dad to interact with their children. The History Channel, the National Geographic Channel, and some public television specials offer intelligent programming the entire family can enjoy.

In 1988, when I was the principal of Purchase School in Harrison, New York, the staff, the PTA, and I enthusiastically endorsed and supported a program called Turn Off the TV Week. My vision and goal of encouraging more and more reading made this program a no-brainer, and I jumped on it like a free trip to Italy. Our book fair was scheduled for the same time, which allowed us to offer books on a wide array of topics and at various reading levels for all our students.

Parents and students agreed to sign a pledge to turn off the TV for one solid week (24-7) and read books instead of watching the tube. More than half our students signed up, and, surprisingly, most of those students completed the full week—a sacrifice made in the name of literacy—despite a drastic change in routine for their entire family.

We required students to maintain a list of the books they read, and asked parents to verify that the students had completed the books by signing off on the reading list. To further encourage our students to participate, we began the week with a book fair and ended the week with an evening book fair, including refreshments for the entire family. Since this was so successful, we held Turn Off the TV Week the following year, and from then on, it became an annual event.

ELECTRONICS GONE WILD

Computers, tablets, digital toys, cell phones, video games, and iStuff are robbing your children of precious learning opportunities. That realization was clearly depicted in one of my favorite comic strips, *Baldo*, created by Hector Cantú and Carlos Castellanos. In this selection, two friends are talking to each other:

Frame 1: "Do you know Lincoln's Gettysburg Address?"
Frame 2: "Oh man, no, I don't."
Frame 3: "But I might have his email address."[6]

The use, or should I say misuse, of electronics is better explained by David Gelernter, a Yale professor of computer science, who is quoted as having said:

"Many [children] will settle down with the latest iStuff, each like a happy dog with a big bone, and all those pads, pods, smartphones, videogame machines and computers look like good, useful fun.

"But look again. We ought to group these machines with alcohol and adult movies. They're fine for grown-ups but no good for children under 13, except for online learning when they're at home and simple cell phones when they go out."

Gelernter also believes that these digital toys represent "a mental purgatory" that harms a child's ability to concentrate.[7]

YOUR SCHOOL'S READING PROGRAM

Ask your child's teacher to explain the school's reading program to you. It is important that you obtain a copy of the school's reading standards and benchmarks—i.e., what your child is required to know and be able to do at her grade level. Keep the copy at home, preferably in your child's portfolio, and discuss the expectations with your child. Seek advice and direction from the teacher, the school's media specialist, and the public or school librarian, if necessary.

Become a member of your school's parent teacher organization. Request that this organization sponsor a program that explains the school's and school district's goals and objectives for K–12 language arts. Staff members, including the principal, can make presentations that address the curriculum grade by grade. These information sessions will provide opportunities to review and discuss the overall curriculum.

The birth of your child should inspire you to raise a reader. Time is of the essence. It's never too late to turn someone on to reading, but later it will be more difficult, as habits will have already begun to form. Try to remain inspired as you direct your child toward a rewarding life filled with great books, a love of reading, and a love of learning. Don't let this opportunity pass you by—so many books, so little time.

As I like to say: Reading is forever—forever enjoyable and forever useful.

CHAPTER 9: I DREAD SUMMER

"Summertime (and the Livin' Is Easy)"
"It Ain't Necessarily So"
—George and Ira Gershwin, *Porgy and Bess* (1935)

Dear Dr. Casale,

I dread summer because I can't afford to send my children to a sleep-away camp, or any place, for that matter. I am a stay-at-home mom and need some advice about how to keep a nine-year-old son and seven-year-old daughter occupied with some learning activities. I am afraid that the long summer vacation will cause them to fall behind in school if they are not doing some kind of schoolwork. Last summer was a disaster. I need some ideas.

Thanks,
Sharon in California

Dear Sharon,

Your sentiments are mirrored in many households across the country, including those of my own grandchildren. Many parents do not look forward to the lazy, hazy days of summer for the reasons you mentioned.

As a former school principal, I have encountered parents who could afford to send their children to sleep-away camp, Grandma's and Grandpa's summer cottage on Cape Cod, and even Bora Bora. These children were usually out of sight within twenty-four hours of the last day of school and did not return until back-to-school flyers dominated the Sunday newspaper ads. Of course, these parents were in the minority.

Most moms and dads were not as fortunate and were seeking other creative alternatives within their own communities before the last bell rang. Working parents had the additional concern of placing their children in a safe and suitable summer environment with trusted adults.

Some of the options available during the lengthy summer break are sports camps, bible schools, library reading programs, school recreation programs, and summer school programs, which are often remedial and provide needed help for those who may be behind in their studies. However, these are limited solutions available for only a week or two at a time. They will not fulfill the June-to-September time frame.

Sincerely,

Dr. Casale

DR. CASALE'S SUMMER ACADEMY

A *Baby Blues* comic strip by Jerry Scott and Rick Kirkman captures the sentiments of moms around the country as summer approaches. Wanda, a young mother, is talking to her own mother on the phone.

Wanda: "I can't take it, Mom! It's too soon!"

Mother: "You'll be fine, Wanda. I survived it, and you'll survive it too."

Kids: "School's almost out! School's almost out!"

Wanda: "But they'll be home *all* summer!"

Mom: "I'll send a goodie box full of cookies and aspirin."[1]

Before the Beginning

If you decide to introduce learning activities into your child's summer vacation, be prepared for the inevitable question "Aw, Mom! Why do we have to read and do school stuff in the summer?" Your answer is simply this: "Because if you want to succeed in school, you cannot take two and a half months off from learning and practicing 'stuff' and expect to be ready for the challenges of the new school year."

Sports analogies may work with both boys and girls. Explain to your children that even when a sports season ends, athletes keep in shape and prepare for the next season by working out to stay in shape and, believe it or not, learning more to improve their performance. Emphasize that winning athletes do not spend all their time between seasons watching TV and relaxing. Here are examples of two dedicated athletes that you can use to encourage your children to continue learning:

After helping the Miami Heat win the 2012 basketball championship, power forward LeBron James joined Team USA, the Olympic basketball team. He continued playing and learning. After the Olympics, LeBron came home to Florida and, along with his teammates, began his summer regimen, which you can view on YouTube. The video shows him keeping in shape and getting ready for the next season by running on the beach, running up and down stairs, and working out at the gym.

Peyton Manning, a Super Bowl–winning quarterback and MVP, reports to the training facility as soon as the season ends. He studies game films and reviews the complicated playbook. Why? He wants to get better. Mentally, he's already preparing for the first kickoff, which is five months away.

Make your summer academy fun! No desks are necessary, and no bells will ring. Since listening to teachers will not be necessary, yawning will be nonexistent. Going to the bathroom and getting a snack will be on an as-needed basis. Your children will say good-bye to tests, pressure to perform, anxiety, boredom, and clock watching and will say hello to excitement and adventure.

While parents will assume the primary role of planners and organizers, children should be allowed to take an active part in choosing activities they consider fun, interesting, and informative. If you make children feel that their opinions count, you can expect cooperation, collaboration, and a positive attitude toward growth activities.

I want to emphasize that parents are not expected to be substitute teachers and that no special skills are needed. You are *not* expected to teach. Your job is to be the activities director—the arranger of things to do. You are expected to provide the conditions for learning: schedule trips, stock the house with learning tools, create or purchase hands-on projects, and set aside quiet time for reading and writing. Limiting television and other electronics is still a good idea in the summer.

Language Arts Take Center Stage

Every summer event, activity, or project presents an opportunity to increase the learning curve by reading, writing, speaking, and listening. Continue to encourage all language skills, and, if possible, become a participant and set the example. Vacations, shopping, day trips, play dates, movies, eating out, gardening, family visits, parties, camps, bird watching, cooking, fishing, swimming, walking the dog, and anything else you can think of has the potential to improve your child's skills in the language arts.

Of course, I am not suggesting that every activity requires an assignment, but I am recommending that children engage at least five days per week in an undertaking that entails reading and writing. A component of this exercise will involve speaking, which usually does *not* have to be encouraged, and listening, which *does* have to be encouraged.

Reread chapter 8 ("Raise a Reader") and chapter 2 ("I Pledge Allegiance"). Stand firm on your insistence that some reading take place five days a week, at the very least. Schools often provide summer reading lists and assignments. Refrain from bribes or any form of tangible rewards. Allow your children to choose what they want to read and write about. Do not insist on chapter books or lengthy writing assignments, but do insist on a regular reading and writing schedule.

Daily writing can be accomplished easily if a journal is part of your child's summer activities. Students normally write in journals at school. If they do not, they should. Journals are invaluable teaching and learning tools. Children can write on topics that interest them or about a recent activity.

Journal writing serves several purposes. Depending on the child's age, it requires that a student read what she or he has written, edit it, and then discuss it. Mom and Dad should make themselves available to listen but not necessarily to critique. With your child's permission, the summer journal should be presented to the teacher at the beginning of the next school year. It will assist the teacher in assessing your child's current writing skills. The only way to improve one's writing is to write.

Start the journal on the first day of summer vacation. The focus is not on the amount of writing but on the ideas and content. Don't worry if your child writes only a few sentences. If your child likes rhyming games, encourage her or him to write poetry. Perhaps something persuasive, like "Why I Need a New Bicycle," or something amusing, "My Life Without Ice Cream," will spark an interest. Ask them to write a movie review or a review of a show you have both watched on television.

Whether your house is filled with quality reading materials or not, schedule a trip to the library each week. Learn the names of the most popular children's books in the appropriate age range for your son or daughter and reserve them in advance from the librarian. Seek advice from the library staff about games, software, videos, and websites. Libraries are free!

Math

Math is so much more than adding, subtracting, multiplying, and dividing. Given today's calculators, doing math by hand is as rare as a truthful politician. I love math and loved teaching math, but it wasn't a subject that came easily to me. I barely got past intermediate algebra in high school. Since the mention of the word *calculus* scared me, I ended my formal study of math by completing the basic requirements. Regardless, I still love its challenging aspect. I sometimes regret not having taken the next step.

In daily life, math is more important for its ability to teach problem solving and critical thinking. Consider purchasing math workbooks, math games, or computer programs. Again, utilize the resources of your local library. Talk to teachers and other parents, and/or go online and research math websites like www.coolmath.com.

Math activities can be incorporated effortlessly into daily life. Cooking presents measuring opportunities, and shopping provides occasions to add, subtract, multiply, divide, estimate, and calculate percentages for taxes.

Check out the Kahn Academy on YouTube. Kahn provides free math instruction. Take advantage of the other resources available online. Don't fret about your own math ability. You are not expected to teach geometry! Seek advice from experts, and be honest with your children about your own abilities. Your child will see that you are not afraid to ask for help—a worthy lesson in itself.

Science/Social Studies/Art/Music/PE

Any subject can be incorporated into your home summer program. If your child has an interest in a specific subject, like science or history, turn her loose. Books, magazines, and websites host a universe of subjects and topics that may inspire your child to read more, learn more, and do more. You may be raising the next Jane Goodall!

Day trips to museums, farms, galleries, nature centers, and aquariums are all learning experiences that may ignite your children's curiosity and lead them in untold directions. Do not force-feed. Tempt. Dangle the carrot by making opportunities and resources available. Set the proverbial table. Include plenty of playtime and exercise.

Electronics Gone Wild Again

The advent of summer may wrongly signal to your child that endless hours of mindless video games, TV, Skype, and texting lie ahead. Burst that bubble quickly and firmly!

The cartoon *Freshly Squeezed*, by Ed Stein, captures this sentiment from the child's point of view with great clarity:

Grandpa: "When I was a kid, every day in the summer we'd get on our bikes, and we'd meet up in the park or at someone's house. And we'd play games or just sit and talk."

Grandson: "Yeah, but . . . that was before email and Skype."[2]

One Last Assignment

My summer academy is not designed to be stressful or create anxiety. Fun is the primary component. Keep it light and enjoyable. If you, as the parent, keep an open mind and a willingness to "share" the adventure, your child will be more receptive and excited as each new day dawns. Pace yourself and leave days when the only important thing you and your child have to do is nothing. Maintaining your sanity is of critical importance.

Now, here is your one and only real assignment. Start a journal of your own. Record your daily plans, activities, and thoughts. Share it with your family and ask for input from your spouse and children. Evaluate your experiences and modify your plan, if necessary.

Stay committed to the task, but be flexible, calm, civil, and patient. Dedicated parents are the most important influence in a child's life. Giving birth left you with no other option than to do your best. No one will ask more.

> "Genius is one percent inspiration and ninety-nine percent perspiration."
>
> —Thomas Edison

CHAPTER 10: HOW IS YOUR CHILD DOING IN SCHOOL?

Alice: "Would you tell me, please, which way I ought to go from here?"

Cheshire Cat: "That depends a good deal on where you want to go to."

Alice: "I don't much care where."

Cheshire Cat: "Then it doesn't matter which way you go."

—Lewis Carroll, *Alice's Adventures in Wonderland*

Do you know what your child is supposed to be doing and learning in school? Are you aware of the expectations for each grade—which skills should be attained and what specific knowledge should be acquired at the conclusion of elementary school, middle school, and high school? If your child is already attending school, are you satisfied with his or her progress? Many parents across this country are not happy, and they are demonstrating it in various ways.

SCHOOL REFORM

"I can't get no satisfaction" is the widely recognized first line from a Rolling Stones classic 1965 hit. This sentiment is driving the school reform movement as parents seek alternatives to the failing public school system. More and more states are expanding their charter school options and voucher programs as parent dissatisfaction increases.

Charter schools are essentially public schools that operate without the restrictive rules and regulations of regular public schools. Charter schools can focus on specific themes, such as science. They are free to revise curricula and management schemes and to fire teachers who are not performing effectively. Charter schools have opportunities to be more creative and innovative. They are more responsive to parental concerns. Equally important, charter schools are not governed by the demands of teachers' union contracts. Teachers' unions do not approve of charter schools. As beneficial as charter schools can be, they are not always successful. There are no guarantees.

The voucher system allows parents to enroll their children in private schools. Vouchers represent a portion of tax dollars that the state school system would normally expend on one child. But it is allotted to parents for private school tuition. Nationally, this system is referred to as *school choice*.

The California Trigger Law, which is spreading to other states, allows parents, by majority vote, to close failing schools or convert them to charter schools. Homeschooling is on the rise, and private school enrollment is increasing.

Much has been written about school reform—it's a topic of intense debate. One important fact emerges that is worth remembering. Student test scores in math and reading have remained stagnant—virtually unchanged—since the 1970s. The role of parents in their children's education remains as critical as ever.

WHO IS TO BLAME?

In his book *Smart Kids, Bad Schools*, Brian Crosby offers a chapter titled "Meet the Worst Teachers: The Parents."[1] Fifty years as an educator in four different states have qualified me to say, "He's right!"

I have witnessed parents slapping their children and cursing them in public. I have seen parents drag their screaming children out of a store. I have seen them bullying their children and being bullied by their children. I have known parents who bribe their children to do their homework and make excuses for every infraction their child commits. These parents come from all socioeconomic levels.

Read the newspaper or watch the news if you need more evidence that parenting skills do *not* come naturally to many people. Even caring and loving parents must learn how to teach, set examples, and inspire their children.

Recently, while dining at my favorite breakfast spot and enjoying my pecan pancakes smothered in maple syrup, I noticed a young mom enter the restaurant with her toddler. They were accompanied by an older woman, whom I suspect was the grandmother. The child carried a humongous toy fire engine, which he promptly placed on the table, leaving almost no room for the food. While this was an inconvenience to the waitress, the adults were not fazed by the lack of room for the food or the potential for an accident.

The mind-boggling responsibility of being a parent comes with no manual and no training. Doctors, lawyers, teachers, dentists, plumbers, and our military not only are trained before they are considered ready for their responsibilities, but need to upgrade their skills and knowledge regularly in order to maintain their edge and do the best they can. Who trains parents?

During my professional career, I attended numerous workshops and conferences on how to become a better teacher and leader. As beneficial as these experiences were, I learned much more from reading professional articles and books, observing highly effective teachers and leaders, asking questions, and trying out what I learned.

How confident are you in your abilities to parent effectively? Could you do better? Of course you could. Learning is a sponge without a saturation point. We can never soak up enough knowledge. You can become what you want your child to be—a lifelong learner. If you haven't already started, get going.

When students don't do well in school, where do we point the finger of blame: at the teacher, at the principal, or at the parents? Sometimes, the answer is all three.

Sadly, many parents refuse to acknowledge their role in their child's lack of progress. Too many moms and dads remain outside the education equation. They are too busy, uninterested, selfish, unsupportive, or ignorant, or, worse, they assume the school will take care of their child's needs.

Children spend the majority of their time outside of school. Who is responsible for monitoring their behavior and their education during those periods? You are. No matter your own frustrations, anxiety, and fatigue, you must make the time to participate in your child's total education. No special skills are necessary.

During the devastating Chicago teachers' strike in September 2012, 350,000 students were without school for seven days. The parents were livid. That's an understandable burden for both working and stay-at-home parents. Fortunately, the public libraries stepped in and helped out by opening their facilities each day to thousands of children.

What was the reason for this strike? You might assume that money was the issue, but you would be wrong. The teachers were complaining less about their salaries and more about being evaluated. One teacher, speaking on behalf of many, complained that their evaluations "did not consider the parent's role in education." For emphasis, the teacher pointed out that many kids came to school unwashed, unfed, uninterested, and unprepared. In other words, parents were part of the problem. The problems in Chicago included failing schools, low graduation rates, poor test scores, and behavioral issues. These are familiar obstacles no matter where you live.

> "One person can shape a child, and that child can shape the world."
> —Anonymous

Who should that one person be? The answer is obvious. No one will serve your child's needs better than you will serve them. No one should care or will care about your child's future more than you do.

LEARNING STANDARDS:
WHAT DO PARENTS NEED TO KNOW?

Before parents can assess how their child is doing in school, they must become familiar with what their child is expected to know and be able to do at his or her grade level. Learning standards are general statements of the outcomes (knowledge and skills) students are expected to master during the year. They represent the framework of each school's and school district's goals and objectives and its written curriculum. The curriculum comprises the material a teacher is expected to cover for a specific grade.

For Example . . .

A learning standard in language arts specified for grades two through four could read as follows: students will read, write, listen, and speak for critical analysis and evaluation.

A reading objective (outcome) states the following: using children's books, articles, advertisements, or an electronic source, the student will be able to evaluate the content by:

- Identifying the author's purpose
- Identifying important details
- Distinguishing between fact and opinion

As a parent, you are entitled to and should seek this information, as well as any further explanations you require to understand what is expected of your child. For example, reading encompasses much more than decoding or sounding out words. Reading progresses from decoding to basic comprehension to analyzing and evaluating information. The goal is to develop critical-thinking skills that will continuously serve the lifelong learner.

Parents are not reading teachers, nor are they expected to be. What is expected is that parents will gather information from the school and use that information to ask questions, observe progress, communicate with the teacher, and make decisions that are in the best interests of their child.

THE PURPOSE OF SCHOOL

Reread chapter 1 and reflect again on your hopes and dreams for your child. Giving your hopes and dreams more specificity may require that you embrace and even record actual goals and objectives that a child of any age can easily discuss and understand.

About fifty-five million kids from kindergarten to twelfth grade returned to school this year. Most have no idea why they are attending school other than "because I have to." Many consider school an opportunity to socialize, play sports, and get out of the house. Others see school as an inconvenient interruption to TV, computers, video games, iPads, and iPods.

I often pose this question to my college students: "What is the purpose of school?" Without fail, their responses can be grouped into two general categories: first, to get an education; second, to prepare for the world of work.

Both of these are generally correct. They do, however, overlook one very fundamental reason for attending school in a democratic republic: learn how to become a good citizen.

WHAT IS A GOOD CITIZEN?

To be good citizens, people must be informed about the issues in their community, their state, and their country. Participating in the decision-making process by voting for our representatives is by far one of the most important requirements of a good citizen. How do we explain this to our children?

Begin by pointing out that a good citizen is an informed and educated citizen. Informed citizens can read critically, write clearly, and understand basic computation. These abilities allow for intelligent participation in the decision-making process that affects one's future. Studying history, geography, science, and the arts helps children understand their communities, their culture, other cultures, their country, the environment, and the world.

Figuring out how to get along with everybody and appreciating and respecting different cultures and the environment will prove to be joyful, useful, and worthwhile as children progress from student to citizen to contributing member of our society. A contributing member of society learns how to respect other people's opinions, evaluate information, solve problems, and make decisions. It's called critical thinking.

No matter the grade level of your child—be it kindergarten or high school—your expectations must be clear and, if necessary, communicated often. Let your children know what you expect, and be there to support their efforts.

SUGGESTIONS

I previously mentioned that it is difficult, if not impossible, to force your child to do something he or she doesn't want to do, such as reading good books or exercising. Please avoid bribery; deprivation of food, water, and sleep; and forcing them to watch silent movies. These tactics may work in the short term but will have long-lasting negative effects. What you can do is *set the table* by creating and sustaining a learning culture in your home. The best method is always to set a good example. Walk the walk!

Sir Ken Robinson, author and professor emeritus at the University of Warwick in the UK, offers this metaphor for parents, in which he encourages them to think of themselves as gardeners:

"Gardeners know that they can't make plants grow. Plants grow themselves. Gardeners provide the right conditions for that to happen. Good gardeners understand those conditions. Raising a family is much more like gardening than like engineering. It's about providing the best conditions for growth and development. And if we get that right, we'll see an abundant harvest of talent, commitment, imagination, and creativity in all our children and in all our schools."[2]

Avoid stress, angst, and frustration. Till the learning garden, set the table for learning, and model your expectations for your children. More will not be asked of you. Children who do not see the light will, hopefully, learn from their mistakes and/or have to accept the consequences of their efforts, which are lessons in themselves.

THE PORTFOLIO, REVISITED

Purchase a large portfolio, the kind that can be secured with a flap and an elastic string. Starting in kindergarten (or right now), maintain a file of your child's schoolwork. Homework, class work, quizzes, tests, projects, complete and incomplete assignments, interim reports, report cards, teacher notes, and parent-teacher-conference notes should be included. This becomes your reference material, maybe a future scrapbook.

Your children's daily work will reveal their strengths, weaknesses, gaps, and progress. The knowledge you gather about the school's expectations via the curriculum and the evidence that you maintain in the portfolio will answer your question "How is my child doing in school?"

If you have questions or need clarification, contact the teacher. Deliver sincere compliments and praise for exemplary work to your child *and* the teacher. Consider maintaining a separate folder to keep those assignments of which your child is most proud.

COMMUNICATION

Use the contents of the portfolio as an opportunity to regularly discuss school and schoolwork with your child. Regular dialogue—daily is best—is a powerful manifestation of your commitment, devotion, and attitude toward learning. It conveys an important message to your child: *I care!*

Use the contents of the portfolio as discussion points at teacher conferences. Do *not* wait for interim reports or report cards from the school. If you feel that you need more information or just reassurance based on what your child is bringing home, contact the teacher. Be proactive. In the land of email, communication and feedback are swift. Most teachers check their email daily and respond to parents within twenty-four hours.

If you are hesitant to contact a teacher because you think he will feel annoyed or put-upon, you are misguided. I always respected the parents who were either in my office or calling me regularly with questions, issues, or problems. Their concerns, while not usually critical or earth-shattering, revealed to me that they were advocates for their child. They expected their child to do well and were monitoring the situation.

HIGH-STAKES TESTING

Annual standardized tests are not necessarily an indication of how well your child is progressing. These exams should never be the only determiner of progress. Often outsourced by states to private companies that design them, standardized tests are not always valid or reliable measures of what students have learned.

Some students are not good test takers, especially given the anxiety that accompanies the boot camp mentality that often precedes test week. Physical, emotional, and mental health may play a big part in the results. Conversely, when students score well on these exams, we automatically assume they have mastered their subjects. Again, I quote from the great American opera *Porgy and Bess*: "It ain't necessarily so."

Teachers are not fond of standardized tests. All too often, the results are used to evaluate a teacher's performance for the entire year. This is a contentious issue among teachers, school districts, and SEDs (state education departments). Teachers feel that they are forced to teach to the test, rather than the curriculum standards. School districts want these quantitative results to judge the performance of each teacher, because it is an easy way for the uninformed to make determinations of effectiveness. A comprehensive evaluation system that includes test results as one of the components may be the answer to this issue. Teacher evaluation protocols remain a topic of intense debate throughout the country.

Annual test results are not the sole responsibility of a particular teacher. They are the cumulative result of all the preceding teachers and school experiences that your child has had up to that grade. Did it ever occur to you that if your child had a different teacher, results might be different? High-stakes tests and even report cards are more subjective than you may think.

Additionally, you must factor in your own role and responsibility as an involved parent. Did you set the table for learning? Did you prepare the soil, as Sir Ken Robertson recommends? You are the headmaster in charge of the learning environment at home. Did you do your job? You are accountable.

The team approach to learning—family and school working together—is your child's best chance at success. It doesn't "take a village" unless *you* are the village.

> "The smallest school in America is the family."
> —John Gardner

CHAPTER 11: THE PARENT REPORT CARD

Feedback Is the Breakfast of Champions

How Am I Doing?

Ed Koch, the former mayor of New York City, while strolling through the streets of Manhattan, was reportedly fond of asking passersby "How am I doing?" I don't recall how anyone responded, but I never forgot what this simple gesture represented. He knew he would be held accountable, and he was seeking feedback on how well he was fulfilling the responsibilities of his job.

Earlier in this book, I took the liberty of reminding parents of the enormous and sacred responsibility they have assumed as their children's first and most influential teachers. A parent's love, care, understanding, protection, knowledge, and guidance provide the foundation upon which a child blossoms and unfolds into a person who becomes an admirable citizen—caring, respectful, responsible, and literate.

Whether they realize it or not, parents need feedback. Everyone does. How else can we improve? A job of this magnitude and significance is a 24-7 responsibility unlike any other. Successful parenting requires periodic assessment and evaluation if we are to accurately measure our progress.

My Parent Report Card is designed to stimulate and guide you. Not only does it require Mom and Dad to evaluate their own efforts, it provides insight into the process of raising a family in a culture of learning.

SHORT AND SIMPLE

Relatives of mine, who have no children, have this sign posted in their home: THIS HOUSE IS DESIGNED FOR THE COMFORT AND PLEASURE OF OUR DOGS.

I love dogs, and I love the sign. It clearly and emphatically states my relatives' priorities. I have witnessed their devotion to their dogs many times. The dogs are healthy, well behaved, and affectionate—although they are a bit smelly.

If you are considering making a sign for your own house, here is a possible choice: THIS HOUSE IS OCCUPIED BY A FAMILY WHO CARES DEEPLY FOR EACH OTHER. WE ARE COMMITTED TO MUTUAL RESPECT, ACCEPTING RESPONSIBILITY FOR OURSELVES, AND THE VALUE OF BECOMING LIFELONG LEARNERS.

FOUR TYPES OF FEEDBACK

Primarily, the object of your love, patience, compassion, hard work, and spending habits is your children. They are always a source of feedback, even when you haven't asked for it and don't want to know. Whether you like it or not, they can and will provide you with a variety of suggestions and advice on your efforts as a parent and how those efforts are affecting them. Expect some whining and complaining and a few tears. Do not feel obligated to defend your actions. Instead, model good listening and be open to their suggestions. Always set the proper example—it's part of your plan. Your mission statement guides your plan.

A second source of feedback is your child's teacher. Share your mission statement and ask for advice on how to transform your home into a learning center. Confirm and clarify with the teacher what is expected of you in the teacher-parent and teacher-school relationship. It will be included on your report card.

A teacher may or may not be able to assess what is actually going on at home without being there, but your child's improvement and progress at school will indicate that you are an active participant in the learning process. Based on the progress your child is making, a teacher can easily assess the level of cooperation, communication, and collaboration that exists between home and school.

Teachers keep records of everything school related, including attendance at parent conferences. Teachers know when school forms are returned in a timely manner. Teachers also notice which parents follow up on suggestions for their child's improvement. Here is a little tip that will help form a positive relationship with the teacher: never speak to the principal about an issue you have with the teacher before you have spoken to the teacher. Teachers hate that.

A third opportunity for Mom and Dad to evaluate their performance is self-reflection. All highly effective people review their actions, thoughts, and efforts with a critical eye on the following question: Could I/we have done better?

Try to spend a little time each day reflecting on what you have or have not accomplished. Did today's interactions with your children meet your goals? Is a tweak or simple modification necessary? Do you need some advice from a teacher or other expert? Are you modeling what you expect from your children?

Being successfully reflective is best achieved in a quiet and drama-free environment where Mom and Dad can talk to each other or in solitude. Use a journal to record your thoughts, issues, and solutions. Date all entries.

Finally, in keeping with the tradition of school report cards, grade yourself using the criteria I have designed for this purpose. I have designed a report card that represents what parents are expected to know and be able to do, based on the information presented in this book.

Since you are filling out your own report card, honesty is the best policy. Sign it, date it, and share it with your child. Complete your report card using the same schedule that schools use for issuing report cards.

CASALE RESIDENCE LEARNING CENTER
100 Book Street
Successville, Florida 10010-9999
PARENT REPORT CARD

School Year _____ **Quarter** _____

Attitude/Effort   **Yes/No (Y/N)**

(Y/N)

(I) (We) (Our/My) (circle your answer)

- Understand my/our responsibility as first teachers and role models Y/N
- Maintain and display a positive attitude about the importance of learning and school Y/N
- Try my/our best each day to follow my/our plan Y/N
- Remain calm, civil, patient, and loving Y/N

Pledge/Mission Statement

- Wrote my/our pledge or mission statement Y/N
- Shared it with family members Y/N
- Posted it in the house where it can be seen and referenced Y/N
- Will modify it if necessary Y/N

Safety/Security/Discipline

- Have a copy or are fully aware of the school's safety/security/ discipline protocols Y/N
- Toured the school or talked to school officials about safety concerns Y/N
- Wrote and posted house rules that focus briefly on expected behavior and conduct Y/N

- Are aware or have a copy of the teacher's classroom rules, expectations, and consequences Y/N
- Understand the concept of bullying and have discussed it with family members Y/N

Highly Effective Teachers
- Recognize the characteristics of outstanding teachers Y/N
- Appreciate their difficult and challenging work and take the time to support and compliment them Y/N
- Will contact them directly if issues or concerns arise and will never go behind their back Y/N

Reading
- Filled my/our house with good books and other reading materials Y/N
- Read in front of my/our children Y/N
- Established a regularly scheduled reading time at least four times a week Y/N
- Joined the public library Y/N
- Require journal writing at least four times a week Y/N
- Limit TV, video games, and other electronics during school nights Y/N
- Know the expectations of the school's reading program Y/N

Monitoring Progress
- Obtained copies of the school curriculum in each subject Y/N
- Have read the learning standards and objectives for each subject Y/N
- Maintain a portfolio of all schoolwork Y/N

- Regularly discuss schoolwork and progress, especially during the week Y/N
- Maintain regular contact with teachers regarding questions, clarifications, concerns, or compliments Y/N

Summertime
- Are planning to incorporate learning opportunities and activities as an important part of the summer break Y/N
- Will reread chapter 9 before summer vacation Y/N

Signature _____ Date _____

Grade based on number of "yes" answers:

28–30	=	Excellent
23–27	=	Very good
19–26	=	Satisfactory
Below 19	=	Help needed

PART 2: LETTERS . . . I GET LETTERS

"Letters, we get letters
We get stacks and stacks of letters."

—Perry Como

As part of my website format, I ask readers to submit questions, concerns, or comments about the blogs I post. The following questions were submitted to me via my website, www.parentsfirst.biz.

The questions have not been edited for content, but the names of the writers, people, and schools within the letters, as well as my responses, have been changed for privacy considerations. Some responses have been updated.

CHAPTER 12: BILLY HATES MUSIC CLASS

Dear Dr. Casale,

I received a letter from my son's music teacher. The teacher is concerned because Billy is not participating appropriately. When I asked Billy about it, he said he hated music class and didn't care if he got an "N." When I asked him why he hated music class, he said because the teacher makes each student sing alone and he hates singing, especially singing alone. He says it's embarrassing. The teacher asked me to talk to my son or arrange for a conference. I think you should know that my son is very shy but loves music. He takes guitar lessons. What do you think I should do?

Cathy in Fairfield, CT

Dear Cathy,

Should Billy be required to sing solo in front of his classmates? My answer is "no," but I do suggest that you schedule a conference as soon as possible, and bring Billy along as a participant. Bring a notepad and pencil, write down some questions you may have for the teacher, and remember to remain civil, calm, positive, and open-minded.

When you meet with the music teacher, ask if singing solo is a required component of the music curriculum. If it is, ask to see it and have the teacher explain the rationale for singing solo in front of the class. Whether singing is or isn't a requirement, explain Billy's dilemma and ask if he could be assigned an alternative assignment, such as playing the guitar in class, completing a short written report on singing, writing an original song, or reading the words to his favorite song in front of the class. The teacher should have picked up on this already.

Discuss those alternatives with Billy *before* the conference and remind him that an alternative assignment will be required if the teacher agrees to it. If the teacher remains adamant that singing solo is a requirement, see the principal for possible arbitration. There are, of course, no guarantees, and Billy may have to accept an "N" for that marking period.

This is not a crisis situation. As the saying goes, "This, too, shall pass" and may result in a learning experience for all involved.

I do not believe that any teacher in any subject should force a child to perform a task that the child considered embarrassing or demeaning. Would his reading teacher force him to read aloud in front of the class if that were one of his weaknesses and it embarrassed him?

Teachers are expected to be more sensitive and knowledgeable, and they usually are. The great teachers are all of the above, as well as being creative. They can easily assess these situations and devise alternatives to accommodate specific situations.

I am not advocating that you intervene in every situation that your child finds unacceptable. Be very careful, use common sense, trust your instincts, and seek advice. Your child must learn to navigate uncomfortable situations or learn how to accept the consequences. It is a learning opportunity that will serve him well in the future.

CHAPTER 13: PROFANITY IN MY DAUGHTER'S ASSIGNED BOOK

Dear Dr. Casale,

[Is it] normal for tenth graders to be reading books with profanity in them? Like #@*&$, curse words, like *+%$@$^^$#&(&&%. Very explicit talk about sex? I sure as hell wasn't assigned to read those types of books at Catherine's age! My daughter is not in favor of a conference with the teacher but did admit to some embarrassment when asked to read the passages aloud.

Joyce in Bridgeport, CT

Dear Joyce,

Ignore your child's request about scheduling a conference. Do not include her in the conference, since she may feel embarrassed. Feel free to tell the teacher that your child was not in favor of the conference but that you have serious concerns about the book that was chosen to be read aloud in class. As always, write your thoughts and questions before you arrive at the conference, bring a notepad and take notes on what is discussed, remain calm and civil.

If possible, bring your spouse to the meeting; two parents can be more effective than one. Be prepared to do the following:

• Bring the book with you and note the objectionable parts.

- State unequivocally that this language is not tolerated in your home, and your child will not participate in this book's activities.
- Inquire about school district guidelines or standards regarding the use of this type of profane and sexual material.
- Ask how this book was chosen to be included in the curriculum.
- Ask about the learning objective this book was serving and could there have been other choices.
- Seek an alternative assignment for your daughter.

If you're not satisfied, repeat 1–6 with the principal. Follow the chain of command after that if you are not satisfied.

I am not an advocate of book banning, nor am I prudish, but I am an advocate of good taste and common sense. In our society, beauty is in the eye of the beholder, and so is art or what passes for art. Normally community standards determine what is acceptable as good literature. Some communities have banned *Huckleberry Finn* due to what is now considered racist language.

There are enormous amounts of highly acclaimed literary works that may benefit high school students and meet curriculum objectives. I would ask myself how this book was chosen and what literary value it reveals. Do *not* fall for the following defensive responses by educators:

- It was recommended by our curriculum coordinator.
- A nearby community uses it.
- It's age appropriate.
- What's the big deal? These kids watch R- and X-rated movies and actually use this kind of language.

- It was on the book list sent home at the beginning of the year.

When parents feel strongly about a school issue that affects their children and/or their community, they can set an example by investigating the issue and then making determinations about a course of action. Knowledge is power, but knowledge alone does not translate into results. If parents seek change, they must become knowledgeable and proactive.

Think this through. Do not be intimidated. You know how you feel and you have a right to express your feelings.

CHAPTER 14: MISSING IN ACTION

Dear Dr. Casale,

My third-grade daughter recently has been bringing home sub-par work in reading. Her work last year was satisfactory. She does receive extra help in reading from the school's reading specialist. I scheduled a conference with the classroom teacher and the reading specialist but the reading specialist did not show up. The conference with the regular teacher did not go well. She not only seemed uninterested but indicated that she did not offer reading instruction to my child. I left the conference angry and upset that I was not being informed about a lack of progress. My daughter also tells me that when she gets something wrong, the teacher gets mad. I will appreciate your advice.

Mark, Palm City, FL

Dear Mark,

Since perception is reality, your dissatisfaction is real. There are several options from which to choose:

- Make an appointment with the principal, bring your child's work, and express your dissatisfaction.
- Call the reading specialist and inquire about her absence. Possibly there was some miscommunication.

- Reschedule a conference with both teachers.
- Reschedule with only the reading specialist.

Before scheduling a conference, reread my article on parent conferences. Consider bringing your daughter to the conference of your choice. I would advise seeing the principal first before rescheduling with the reading teacher. Always bring prepared questions to a conference, and a notebook. Take notes on what is said and decided.

Maintain a portfolio of your child's work at every grade and in every subject. The portfolio also includes report cards, standardized testing data, quizzes, tests, correspondence, and notes from conferences. Make sure you are seeing daily classwork on a regular basis—at least once a week.

Assume some responsibility for growth in reading and make it a family priority. Fill your house with books, set aside a quiet time— free of distractions—each night for reading and journal writing, and model your own interest in reading by reading regularly at the same time. Limit TV, video games, and any other electronics that distract students from their studies.

You are on the right track. Remain concerned and active in your child's education. Get the facts and learn as much as you can about the goals and objectives of each course of study. Work cooperatively with teachers in a calm, civil, positive, but determined manner.

CHAPTER 15: I THINK MY CHILD IS GIFTED

Dear Dr. Casale,

I encountered problems with my son's teacher and school officials regarding their gifted program. They are resisting my efforts to get my son tested. I know he is gifted *and* he is not being challenged in his regular classroom. What can I do about this?

Maggie, Westport, CT

Dear Maggie,

Normally, there is a discrete set of protocols within each school district that outline the screening, testing, and placement of gifted students. Accommodating gifted students is a component of ESE—Exceptional Student Education—the same component that places students with disabilities. To the best of my knowledge, gifted programs focus mainly on the cognitively gifted student and not those whose talents are demonstrated in other intelligences as defined by developmental psychologist Howard Gardner.

The initial recommendation for entry to a gifted program may come from either the parent or the child's classroom teacher, although this may vary with school districts. The process usually begins with a questionnaire completed by the classroom teacher and can include applicable test scores on standardized tests and examples of the student's work. Also included will be in-house testing by the school psychologist, and, finally, all the information is presented and discussed at a formal meeting attended by the parents, classroom teacher, school psychologist, gifted teacher, and principal. The meeting determines whether the child has met the criteria to enter the program. These protocols appear to be fair and objective, but my experience informs me otherwise.

Classroom teachers who are not convinced that the student is gifted can influence the decision making in several ways:

- By being less than objective on the required questionnaire and in their oral presentation
- By bringing work samples to the meeting that are not indicators of the child's ability

Conversely, some outstanding teachers think, and rightly so, that they can provide the challenges needed for any student. I know of a case in which the parent opted out of a gifted program for his son because he felt the regular teacher was more competent than the teacher of the gifted class.

If you truly believe that your child needs the challenges of a gifted program and is qualified, proceed as follows:

- Obtain all needed information from district and school personnel, including a complete description of the gifted curriculum and the criteria for admission.
- Create your own folder with your written observations from home and samples of your child's work. You also may be required to complete a questionnaire.
- Pay attention to deadlines, both yours and those of school officials.

- Follow up. Follow up. Follow up. Ask questions and communicate with school officials.
- Some parents have opted to have their child tested privately as a source of information and data. This may be helpful.
- Move forward with your concerns regarding the regular classroom. You will need concrete examples of the work your child is doing that does not measure up to his ability and what he should be doing. This is often a hard sell, but the more information you can gather, including standardized test results, the better prepared you will be to state your case.

Ultimately your child must test into the program. If the scores do not meet the criteria to enter the program, your child will most likely not be allowed to participate.

CHAPTER 16: NEGATIVE COMMENTS

Dear Dr. Casale,

My son's second-grade teacher writes negative comments about his behavior on his planner, which he brings home each day from school. He can read, and he is very upset. So are we. I think the teacher is nitpicking. Should I go right to the principal and complain?

Pam in Jupiter, FL

Dear Pam,

This is a teacher issue, and most classroom circumstances require that you see the teacher first. If you are not satisfied with your conference, then schedule a meeting with the principal. I believe it was improper and unnecessary to write negative comments on your child's planner. The teacher's concerns should have been shared privately with the child and privately with you via email, phone, or a conference. Here are some guidelines that will help you during any school conference:

- Expect and prepare for a thoughtful and civil discussion. Remain calm and positive.
- Bring the planner with you. Bring your son, too.
- Write down your specific questions and requests and have an extra copy for the teacher.

- Examples: Why do you think my child is misbehaving? Is he bored? Is he sitting next to someone who distracts him? Is anyone else acting out or is it just him? Is he frustrated with the work?
- Please do not write negative comments on my son's planner. Share your concerns with me and my husband via private communication.

- Take notes on what is discussed, both agreements and disagreements.
- Arrange for a follow-up conference or communication within an agreed-upon amount of time—no longer than a week.
- Suggest other forms of communication, such as emails or phone calls.

Please inform me as to the results of the conference and let me know if I can be of further assistance.

CHAPTER 17: MY SON HAD
A MISERABLE YEAR IN FOURTH GRADE

Dear Dr. Casale,

My child had a miserable year in fourth grade. He did not like school and he did not like his teacher, who he described as, "She only likes the smart kids." He fell behind and had to receive remediation in a pull-out program. I did not know what to do. How can I avoid this in the future?

David in Black Rock, CT

Dear David,

Whether your child's perception of the teacher is or is not accurate, it is still an important consideration. These disconnects are neither the teacher's fault nor the student's fault. Conflicts occur for a variety of complicated social and/or psychological reasons. For both adults and children, perception plays a part in all of our interactions, not just at school, but also in all settings, such as family, playgroups, clubs, and sports.

That being said, I believe it is the parent's responsibility to catch this mindset early and try to work it out. As soon as parents get a "whiff" of conflict, they should arrange to see the teacher, because if the situation does not improve, their child is in for a long-term negative experience. Do not be complacent. Don't wait for an issue to emerge. Establish a regular routine of two-way communication with the teacher. I advise a weekly schedule of exchanging information.

If the situation does not improve, there are few realistic options. Occasionally, but reluctantly, a principal will move a child to another classroom. Principals do not like to do this for several reasons:

- The move may overload another class.
- It sets a precedent for other parents, who will expect similar consideration.

Unfortunately, if these occasional disconnects emerge during the elementary school years, the student may regress instead of making progress. The effect on the home life can be devastating. Students in middle school or high school may find it easier to cope with these situations and navigate past teachers they do not like, but it's more challenging for elementary students. However, teachers are accountable and so are parents and students.

Finally, I advise parents in these situations, who feel powerless and frustrated, to do the following:

- Schedule a conference. Bring your son.
- Remain calm, civil, and persistent. This situation can normally be solved.
- Monitor the situation carefully until it improves. These disconnects are rare but do happen.
- Maintain a portfolio of all of your child's work.
- Communicate weekly with the teacher. Discuss your feelings and the perceptions your child has about school. Seek strategies for improvement to be used at school and at home.

- Encourage your child at home without criticizing the teacher.
- Become informed about the requirements of the curricula. Obtain copies from the teacher or principal in each subject. These will help you in future discussions with the teacher regarding progress.
- Teachers are not required to please every student, but they are required to create a fair, respectful, and positive learning environment, where students feel valued and safe.
- Seek advice from other education professionals.
- If things do not get better, see the principal and request a different placement.

CHAPTER 18: MISPLACED AND BORED

Dear Dr. Casale,

My grandson, a first grader, was identified by his kindergarten teacher as average. He was placed in first grade in the middle-to-low reading group. He became unruly [and] bored and got in trouble. When the first-grade teacher figured out that he was misplaced, she moved him to the highest reading and math group. He did splendidly after that.

Gail in Arizona

Dear Gail,

This is not an unusual occurrence, especially at the primary level, where test data is scarce or nonexistent and teachers may be prone to rely on subjective data to make decisions. Students can be identified incorrectly for a variety of reasons, ranging from personality issues, to immaturity, to socialization issues. Another variable may be an inexperienced or incompetent teacher.

If none of the above applies, the error may be related to the kindergarten curriculum and/or school placement protocols that require a kindergarten teacher to place students in a grade-one reading group without objective data. Normally, formal reading instruction begins in grade one, and first-grade teachers are usually very capable at identifying readiness for reading. There are diagnostic instruments that assist in their determinations.

I am glad this all worked out on a positive note, but it does reveal how important it is for parents to get involved. I recommend that parents follow these guidelines throughout their child's K–12 experience:

- Communicate early and often with your child's teacher.
- Take notes, ask questions, and be prepared.
- Never assume anything. Monitor progress.
- Maintain a portfolio of your child's work in each subject at every grade level.
- Support the teacher and the school, but assume your sacred responsibility as your child's first teacher and advocate.
- Embrace the importance of lifelong learning, model it, live it, and establish a culture of learning in your home.

CHAPTER 19: ANXIOUS ABOUT MIDDLE SCHOOL

Dear Dr. Casale,

My son is entering middle school this year, and I am very anxious about it. My friends feel the same way. Do you have any suggestions for us?

Mary Ann in Naples, FL

Dear Mary Ann,

I never tell parents not to worry, because that would be fruitless. It would be like telling the sun not to rise. Parents are entitled to worry; it's in their DNA. I have four grandchildren and I am still a worrier. Worry is OK, but anxiety is not healthy.

Your anxiety is common and shared by many parents across the country. My first suggestion is *not* to transfer your anxiety to your son. The famous poet and essayist Robert Louis Stevenson said, "Keep your fears to yourself, but share your courage with others."

From my recent experience as a full-time teacher in the Florida public school system (2009–2010), I learned that students were excited about becoming sixth graders, but the parents were anxious. Going from the "looked up to" group in elementary school to the "looked down at" group in middle school can sometimes be a cause for concern. The transition becomes part of their life experiences and enhances their learning curve. Middle school represents another important opportunity for students to grow and mature and adjust. Life is full of these situations—freshman year in high school and college, a new job, or boot camp in the military.

These next steps should be viewed and anticipated with excitement. They are the next great adventure to be shared by both you and your son.

School districts often attempt to mitigate the anxiety felt by parents and students by providing orientation opportunities near the end of fifth grade. Middle schools often conduct these orientations, which consist of "what to expect" seminars, explaining routines, rules, procedures, and policies.

Student orientations are often more elaborate than orientation meetings for parents. They may include presentations by older middle school students and may allow newcomers to "buddy" with a sixth grader in order to experience the routines of middle school.

Many elementary schools departmentalize several subjects beginning in fifth grade in order to introduce students to the standard middle school structure of having a different teacher for each subject.

Leaving the nurturing cocoon that usually envelops elementary students and forging ahead into an environment that may require more rigor, independence, self-discipline, and adjustments is a ritual and should be an enjoyable experience as children enter puberty and prepare for their teenage years.

There is one caveat to my "Don't worry! Be happy!" attitude. If you have specific concerns about the school your child is scheduled to attend, make an appointment with the principal and share those concerns. I followed my own advice when my son was about to enter middle school. If you do make an appointment with the principal, prepare for the meeting ahead of time with written questions. Take notes during the visit. Do not jump to conclusions; remain positive and always calm and civil.

In summary, think about middle school and beyond as a positive growth experience. Remain committed to your goals and the action plan you have devised to maintain a culture of learning in your home. Work cooperatively with teachers and the school, but do not rely on them. The smallest but most important and influential school is the family. The responsibility and accountability for that school is enormous. Your focus is knowledge, commitment, and action.

CHAPTER 20: THE IMPACT OF VIDEO GAMES

Dear Dr. Casale,

What impact do you think video games and other forms of electronics have on our children?

Francis in Wesley in Chapel, FL

Dear Francis,

Video games, TV, cell phones, and other electronic devices steal valuable time from those children who use these devices excessively, compulsively, or, at worst, addictively. Did you know that seventy-two percent of US citizens between the ages of six and forty-four play video games at least eighteen hours a week? Extreme players engage in these inane games fifty hours a week. Eight percent of game players—mostly boys between the ages of eight and eighteen—are clinically addicted. The symptoms of playing these games excessively include the following:

- lack of motivation and direction
- difficulty facing obligations
- boredom

While I may be several generations removed from today's students, I have firsthand knowledge of the electronics craze. I taught fifth graders during the 2009–2010 school year. Additionally, two of my four grandchildren—both boys—are somewhere between excessive and addicted. (Please do not tell my children I said this.)

Children will be better served by reading, playing with friends, and getting exercise outside, doing their homework, completing school projects, interacting with family, visiting the library, and, if you are lucky, helping around the house. The social ramifications of excessive and compulsive use of electronic devices are alarming.

In extreme cases, children isolate themselves from family and friends and eschew daily routines. Socializing skills cannot be learned or improved by sitting for hours on end—even with a friend—playing these pointless and often disturbing and violent games.

When I was a kid, we hung out on the street corner or at the park. The next generation hung out at the mall. Now kids are hanging out on social networking sites! Yikes! If electronic devices are used for educational purposes, they make sense. If not, they are counterproductive and unhealthy.

Did I mention the violence associated with video games? The violence portrayed in cartoons, TV, rap music, and movies may be considered small change compared to what kids are viewing when they play video games that glorify violence and destruction. I believe that the violence and destruction exhibited in this type of so-called entertainment may contribute to increased violence and crime in our society.

Every article I read about the possible causes of the Sandy Hook tragedy mentioned the pernicious effects of video games.

My advice includes:

- Have a written family plan that limits TV and computer time on school nights unless it is for educational purposes.

- Cell phones for children under sixteen should be used for emergencies or talking to family members only.
- School-night routines must include reading and writing activities whether they are part of a homework assignment or not. Parents should read, too.
- Make family discussions a daily occurrence.
- Allow for plenty of exercise, playtime, and hanging out with friends.
- Everyone contributes to household chores: making beds, setting the table, loading and unloading the dishwasher, walking and picking up after the dog, folding clothes, washing the floor, dusting, doing yard work, filling the salt shaker, and anything else that contributes to a smooth-running household.
- Fill your house with good books and family board games.
- *X* out the Xbox.

The video game problem is a huge topic that is worth investigating. There was an attempt—I believe in California—to ban certain video games because of the disturbing content. It failed the First Amendment test. Remember, in your house, *you* are the Constitution. You are the law. Be a calm but benevolent dictator who serves the best interests of your children.

CHAPTER 21: SARCASM IN THE CLASSROOM

Dear Dr. Casale,

Ted's fourth-grade teacher is new to the school, just like Ted. Ted's learning style is harder than most. He is a visual learner. The teacher is willing to work with him, but my concern is at times he can be sarcastic. I was able to observe the class for the first time today, as Ted has been struggling. He's been tuning out in class. I am afraid he doesn't want to interact because he's afraid the sarcasm will be the response. Ted has a very soft heart and when things are said to him in such a way, he turns them inward and is so deflated. For example, I was helping him with his homework, and when I told him to redo his letter "F" because it looked like a pretty palm tree, he looked at me and said, "Mom, when you say that it hurts me." I just about died. The light bulb turned on for me. How do I approach this teacher with peace, grace, and respect without throwing a Psychology 101 book at him? Or myself, for that matter. Please understand that in no way am I putting the entire fault on the teacher. We are all working together to light that fire under Ted because school just doesn't come easy for him. But I do feel at the rate it is going, Ted is just going to keep sinking and his academic confidence will be zilch! Any advice would be so appreciated.

Your Asian connection,
Carmel in Ho Chi Minh City, Vietnam

Dear Carmel,

The long and short answer is that sarcasm by a teacher is unacceptable in any form. Sometimes teachers are trying to be funny but it comes across as sarcastic. What may be funny to one child may be hurtful to another. Even teasing or what may be interpreted as "kidding around" with a student may cause a student to feel uncomfortable. Most teachers are very sensitive about this topic and choose their words carefully. Other teachers are not as sensitive.

Unfortunately, there is no way around what you have to do. Do it peacefully, gracefully, and respectfully, but tell the teacher that sarcasm is not acceptable to you or your son, and it is having a negative effect on Ted. If you want change, you are required to express your feelings. Polite and civil discourse and expressing your feelings are not mutually exclusive. Do it as soon as possible.

In the wonderful book *Words That Hurt, Words That Heal,* Rabbi Joseph Telushkin reminds us that we choose our clothes more carefully than we choose our words. While children's behavior can often frustrate parents and teacher, he also suggests that we take the *high road* when interacting with others.

Words are powerful and should not be used to cause psychological or emotional havoc. Teachers and parents are expected to set an example for children, who will learn more by observing than being lectured. Again, make your wishes known to the teacher, and do it in person.

CHAPTER 22: CHALLENGE MY SON

Dear Dr. Casale,

My son is in the Custis Elementary School System second grade. He is very strong in reading and math. I would not say a gifted kid, but a motivated one that does not mind being challenged. I do a lot of work with him at home with reading and using the Miquon math books for his age level. The schoolwork he is getting seems to be just so easy for him, and he blows through it. He has mentioned to me that it is really easy, and he does not seem to be challenged. How can I approach the school to see if they can do more for him? I don't want to overload him but I just want to make sure that he stays interested and challenged. He just started second grade and he read ten chapter books this summer, understands how to multiply numbers and use a ruler. He really gets it when it is presented to him.

Thanks.
Marco in White Plains, NY

Dear Marco,

Your question raises a very common and legitimate concern among parents. I have had several questions on this topic. The outstanding teacher not only knows what to do with accelerated students, but also knows what to do with all students at various stages of ability and motivation. Any given classroom includes students with a wide variety of skills, abilities, motivation, and parental support. Your interest in your child's education is exactly what my blog is about: encouraging parents to become knowledgeable, committed, and involved.

The tendency of the mediocre and less-competent teacher is to teach to the middle of the pack—everybody is on page 72 and everybody is assigned the same basic assignment. But not only do superior teachers have a repertoire of thoughtful and creative strategies to present to accelerated students, they have an arsenal of enrichment materials that will accommodate and challenge students at their level of ability and skills and beyond.

Master teachers have high expectations for all students, and each student should be accommodated based on their developmental level. Based on your letter, your son is ready for more demanding work.

I have heard some teachers tell parents that they are not allowed to proceed beyond the stated curriculum or that the school does not supply them with enrichment materials. This is pure nonsense; do not accept it. Teachers are expected to know how to accommodate accelerated students, provide enrichment materials, and have resources such as computer programs, various websites, and district-wide specialists who can guide teachers toward accommodating advanced students. For example, if I were a teacher struggling with how to better serve accelerated students, I would contact the district's reading specialist, math specialist, other grade-level teachers, or teachers of the academically gifted. Some of the options available to a student who needs to be challenged are:

- Tasks that require higher-order thinking skills, such as evaluating and analyzing topics.
- Opportunities to choose different tasks to accomplish stated objectives. These tasks may require the use of a variety of

resources ranging from books and videos to research and interviews.

- Opportunities to choose their own challenging assignments among those presented by the teacher.
- Activities that require sharing (via presentations) their work and knowledge with their peers.

None of my suggestions should be translated to mean extra work for your son. If your son is finding his schoolwork too easy, the teacher is expected to vary his assignments in a thoughtful and creative way. His work should reflect his current ability and guide him to the next challenging level. I would be surprised if your son was the only student in his class who needed more challenging work.

I advise you to do the following:

- Obtain a copy of the second-grade curriculum in math and language arts. Read it and prepare any questions you may have for the teacher regarding content, objectives, and activities.
- Maintain a portfolio of your son's work.
- Schedule a conference. Bring his work, your questions and concerns, and a notepad to take notes in. Read my article on parent conferences *before* the meeting.
- Confer with other professionals.
- Please keep me apprised of the progress or inroads you are able to make with this situation.

I like to end my letters by inviting the parents to keep in touch. This invitation applies in a broader sense, too. I hope that the information in these pages encourages you to stay as connected as possible to the world your child encounters, at home as well as beyond.

BIBLIOGRAPHY

A Nation at Risk: The Imperative for Educational Reform. United States Department of Education, Washington, D.C., 1983.

Alexandria, VA: Association for Supervision and Curriculum Development, 1988.

American Heritage Dictionary. 2nd ed.

Anderson, Richard C. *Becoming a Nation of Readers: The Report of the Commission on Reading.* Washington, DC: National Academy of Education, 1985.

Brill, Steven. *Class Warfare: Inside the Fight to Fix America's Schools.* New York: Simon & Schuster, 2011.

Brooks, David. "The New Normal." *Palm Beach Post.* March 2, 2011.

Bureau of Justice Statistics (BJS). 2013. http://bjs.ojp.usdoj.gov/index.cfm?ty=dcdetail.

Cantú, Hector. *Baldo. Palm Beach Post.* May 1, 2012.

Centers for Disease Control and Prevention. "Adolescent and School Health." Accessed June 7, 2012. http://www.cdc.gov/HealthyYouth/states/locals/ma-boston.htm.

Christensen, Clayton M. "How Will You Measure Your Life?" *Harvard Business Review* 88, no. 7/8 (July/August 2010): 46–51.

Coleman, James S. *Equality of Educational Opportunity.* Washington, D.C.: U.S. Dept. of Health, Education, and Welfare, Office of Education, 1966.

Covey, Stephen R. *The 7 Habits of Highly Effective People: Powerful Lessons in Personal Change.* New York: Fireside Books, 1990.

Crosby, Brian. *Smart Kids, Bad Schools: 38 Ways to Save America's Future.* New York: Thomas Dunne Books, 2008.

Curwin, Richard, and Allen N. Mendler. *Discipline with Dignity.* Alexandria, VA: Association for Supervision and Curriculum Development, 1988.

135

Cushner, Kenneth, Averil McClelland, and Philip Safford. *Human Diversity in Education: An Intercultural Approach.* 7th ed. New York, NY: McGraw-Hill, 2011.

Dietel, Ronald J. *Get Smart!: Nine Sure Ways to Help Your Child Succeed in School.* San Francisco, CA: Jossey-Bass, 2006.

Fifield, Will. "Teach Your Children Well." *Costco Connection* 27, no. 8 (2012): 32–36.

Garbarino, James, and Ellen deLara. *And Words Can Hurt Forever: How to Protect Adolescents from Bullying, Harassment, and Emotional Violence.* New York: The Free Press, 2002.

Gelernter, David. "Make It a Summer Without iStuff." *Wall Street Journal.* May 10, 2012.

Gerdes, Louise I. Ed. *Cyberbullying (At Issue).* Detroit: Greenhouse Press, 2012.

Glenn, H. Stephen. *Raising Self-Reliant Children in a Self-Indulgent World.* Rocklin, CA: Prima Publishing, 1989.

Goleman, Daniel. *Emotional Intelligence.* New York: Bantam Books, 1995.

Good, Thomas L. *Looking in Classrooms.* New York: Harper & Row, 1973.

Holladay, Jennifer. "Cyberbullying." *Teaching Tolerance* 38 (Fall 2010): 42–45.

"'I'm a monster,' Wayne Treacy laments about beating girl." *Palm Beach Post.* June 4, 2010.

Johnston, Lynn. *Ding Dong Ducky. Palm Beach Post.* 2012.

Johnston, Lynn. *For Better or For Worse. Palm Beach Post.* September 7, 2012.

Klein, Joel. *Lessons of Hope: How to Fix Our Schools.* New York: Harper Collins, 2104.

Kohn, Alfie. *Beyond Discipline: From Compliance to Community.* Alexandria, VA: ASCD, 1996.

Levine, Arthur, "The Suburban Education Gap." *Wall Street Journal.* November 2012.

Marzano, Robert J. *Dimensions of Thinking: A Framework for Curriculum and Instruction.*

Mischel, Walter. *The Marshmallow Test: Mastering Self-Control.* New York: Little Brown & Co., 2014.

"Middle School Fight Recorded on Camera Phone." *Palm Beach Post.* January 2011.

National Assessment Governing Board. *Reading Framework for the National Assessment of Educational Progress: 1998–1992.* Washington, DC: National Assessment Governing Board, 1998.

National Center for Education Statistics home page. http://nces.ed.gov/.

National Center for Education Statistics. "Student Reports of Bullying and Cyber-Bullying: Results from the 2009 School Crime Supplement to the National Crime Victimization Survey." Accessed January 5, 2013. http://nces.ed.gov/pubsearch/pubsinfo. asp?pubid=2011336.

National Education Association. http://www.nea.com/. Accessed October 8, 2015.

O'Moore, Mona, and Stephen James Minton. *Dealing with Bullying in Schools: A Training Manual for Teachers, Parents and Other Professionals.* London: Paul Chapman, 2004.

Schwartz, Heather E. *Cyberbullying.* Minnesota: Capstone Press, 2013.

Scott, Jerry. *Baby Blues. Palm Beach Post.* 2012.

Stein, Ed. *Freshly Squeezed. Palm Beach Post.* July 20, 2012.

StudentsFirst.org. http://www.studentsfirst.org/.

Telushkin, Joseph. *Words That Hurt, Words That Heal: How to Choose Words Wisely and Well.* New York: William Morrow Paperbacks, 1998.

Warren, Richard. *The Purpose Driven Life: What on Earth Am I Here For?* Grand Rapids, MI: Zondervan, 2002.

Wikipedia. "National Crime Victimization Survey." Accessed December 15, 2012. http://en.wikipedia.org/wiki/.

Winkler, Kathleen. *Bullying: How to Deal with Taunting, Teasing, and Tormenting.* Berkeley Heights, NJ: Enslow Publishers, 2005.

NOTES

PART 1

[1] Richard Warren, *The Purpose Driven Life,* page 17.

[2] Stephen R. Covey, *The 7 Habits of Highly Effective People: Powerful Lessons in Personal Change*, page 65.

[3] Will Fifield, "Teach Your Children Well," *Costco Connection* 27, no. 8 (2012), page 35.

[4] The National Commission on Excellence in Education, "A Nation at Risk: The Imperative for Educational Reform," April 1983.

[5] Levine, Arthur. "The Suburban Education Gap." *The Wall Street Journal.* November 2012.

Chapter 1

[1] Richard Rodgers and Oscar Hammerstein collaborated on many musicals that appeared on Broadway and later in the movies.

Chapter 2

[1] http://www.missionstatements.com/school. Accessed October 8th, 2015.

Chapter 3

[1] These recommendations are the result of my own experiences and readings.

Chapter 4

[1] Daniel Goleman, *Emotional Intelligence*, page xii.

[2] Ibid.

[3] Ibid, pages 80-82.

Chapter 5

[1] NCES (National Center for Educational Statistics) http://nces. ed.gov. Accessed October 8, 2015.

[2] Bureau of Justice Statistics

Chapter 6

[1] "'I'm a monster,' Wayne Treacy laments about beating girl," *Palm Beach Post*, June 4, 2010.

[2] Ibid.

[3] National Crime Victimization Survey (2009)

[4] National Education Association (NEA)

[5] Kathleen Winkler, *Bullying*, pages 14-15.

[6] Jennifer Holladay, "Cyberbullying," page 42.

[7] Mona O'Moore and Stephen James Minton, *Dealing with Bullying in Schools*, page 1.

[8] James Garbarino and Ellen deLara, *And Words Can Hurt Forever*, page x.

[9] Ibid.

Chapter 7

[1] www.studentsfirst.org

[2] David Brooks, "The New Normal," *Palm Beach Post*. March 2, 2011.

Chapter 8

[1] National Assessment Governing Board, *Reading Framework for the National Assessment of Educational Progress*, page 1.

[2] Robert J. Marzano, *Dimensions of Thinking*, page 2.

[3] Clayton M. Christensen, "How Will You Measure Your Life?," pages 46-51.

[4] Lynn Johnston, *For Better or For Worse*, *Palm Beach Post*.

5 Alfie Kohn, *Beyond Discipline*, pages 22-25.
6 Hector Cantú, *Baldo*, *Palm Beach Post*. May 1, 2012.
7 David Gelernter, "Make It a Summer Without iStuff," *The Wall Street Journal*. May 10, 2012.

Chapter 9
1 Jerry Scott, *Baby Blues*, *Palm Beach Post*.
2 Ed Stein, *Freshly Squeezed*, *Palm Beach Post*. July 20, 2012.

Chapter 10
1 Brian Crosby, *Smart Kids, Bad Schools*, page 252.
2 Will Fifield, "Teach Your Children Well," *Costco Connection*, pages 32-36.